Professional Resilience:

Helping Doesn't Have to Hurt

Compassion Unlimited Phoenix, AZ
www.forward-facing.com

This book is dedicated to you. All you counselors, law enforcement officers, nurses, social workers, volunteers, physicians, psychologists, correctional officers, mental health professionals, first responders, health care professionals, or anyone who has ever stretched beyond their own comfort to provide care, hope, assistance, and healing for another person. It has been an honor to be in your company these past thirty-five years and share mission with you. I have discovered we are all flawed, scarred, and wounded healers, yet we somehow find the strength, courage, and grit to walk into another day of service. And because you have maintained this fidelity to your purpose and mission, even when it has been painful, you are changing the world one person at a time. Thank you for your service and making the world a little better for me and my family. —EG

Thank you to my friend Gina for showing me what it means to practice with integrity, purpose, and mission and to live according to her values, and starting this journey with me. —MM

About the Authors

J. Eric Gentry, PhD, LMHC, is an internationally recognized leader in the study and treatment of compassion fatigue. His PhD is from Florida State University, where he studied with Professor Charles Figley, who wrote *Compassion Fatigue: Coping with Secondary Traumatic Stress Disorder in Those Who Treat the Traumatized* in 1995. In 1997, under Dr. Figley's direction, Gentry developed the Accelerated Recovery Program for Compassion Fatigue with Anna Baranowsky, PhD, and Kathleen Dunning. The ARP has demonstrated powerful effectiveness for treating the symptoms of compassion fatigue. In 1998, Gentry and Baranowsky introduced the Certified Compassion Fatigue Specialist Training and have trained thousands of professionals towards this designation since that time. Gentry has worked with hundreds of professional caregivers from Oklahoma City, New York City, and the state of Florida following their work with disaster survivors. He has published many research articles, book chapters, and periodicals on the topic of compassion fatigue treatment and resilience. In 2016, he published his groundbreaking book *Forward-Facing Trauma Therapy™: Healing the Moral Wound*. Dr. Gentry draws equally from his scientific study and from his rich history of thirty-five years as a professional therapist to provide this workbook. His commitment to his mission to serve caregivers, helping them to become ever more effective with minimal symptoms, is evident throughout this workbook.

Marette Monson, LCSW, is a well-respected leader in the treatment of compassion fatigue. Mentored by Dr. Gentry, Marette has a private practice called the Center for Counseling Excellence in Salt Lake City, Utah. She focuses on providing treatment to helping professionals who experience compassion fatigue. The Center for Counseling Excellence is one of the only places of its kind in the nation. Marette has extensive knowledge and certifications related to compassion fatigue and trauma. She has authored several articles and has been a nationally sought-after speaker at conferences, on radio shows, and in other media outlets.

Eric and Marette are helping professionals who have experienced compassion fatigue, burnout, and traumatic stress related to the work they do. In this workbook, they mix personal experience, research, and hands-on activities to bring insight and healing with the goal of enabling all helping professionals to continue their work without negative symptoms from it.

Acknowledgement: We would like to thank Marjie Scofield for all the work she put into this workbook.

Table of Contents

Table of Contents

Table of Contents

Education   **Identity**   **Activity**   **Sharing**

Getting the Most Out of This Workbook:

These symbols will help you navigate this workbook quickly. They appear in the margins to direct you to sections designed to build your knowledge, encourage you to identify your own experience, participate in an activity, or share what you have learned with others.

Introduction

Welcome. We are glad you have decided to embark upon this journey with us. Whether you are attending the one-day Professional Resilience and Optimization workshop or just reading this workbook, we hope you enjoy and are enriched by your encounter with this material.

This all began when I (Eric Gentry) started my doctoral program at Florida State University in 1997. I went to FSU to study traumatic stress and its treatment with Professor Charles Figley. I had not even heard the term "compassion fatigue" when I began my studies and work as his research assistant. During that first year of my program, Dr. Figley began the Traumatology Institute through FSU's Center for Professional Development. This was the first training program in the world dedicated to training professionals in treating and serving trauma professionals. I worked with Dr. Figley and other trauma professionals to write and implement the curriculum for the program, and that year it won "training program of the year" through a national continuing education association. Also that year, Dr. Figley had begun The Green Cross as the deployment program arm of the Traumatology Institute. He invited Anna Baranowsky and Kathleen Dunning to Tallahassee to become the first two Green Cross Scholars and participate in development of the training programs and the trauma community that was taking shape at FSU. Anna was finishing her doctorate in clinical psychology at Ottawa University in Canada and Kathleen was a social worker visiting from Port Arthur, New Zealand. We became immediate friends and began working together to help Dr. Figley grow the Green Cross and the Traumatology Institute.

Eighteen months previous, Dr. Figley had released his book *Compassion Fatigue: Coping with Secondary Traumatic Stress Disorder in Those Who Treat the Traumatized*. The publication of this book in 1995, along with Pearlman and Saakvitne's *Trauma and the Therapist* and Beth Stamm's *Secondary Traumatic Stress: Self-Care Issues for Clinicians, Researchers, and Educators*, introduced the concept of compassion fatigue to the general population, and there was much ado about it in Tallahassee. However, must of the discussion about compassion fatigue in 1997 was centered around symptom identification, assessment, and taxonomy. No one had yet to discuss the treatment for this debilitating condition. Kathleen, Anna, and I—wanting to engage in a project together—decided to tackle this initiative, and for the next several months began daily meetings to assemble and test materials and protocols for treating the symptoms of compassion fatigue.

By the summer of 1997, the five-session Accelerated Recovery Program (ARP) for Compassion Fatigue was born. We beta tested the protocol that summer with robust outcome results and were invited to present this model at the International Association for Traumatic Stress Studies annual meeting in Montreal that year. It was pretty exciting for us three students to be thrust into the midst of accomplished professionals to share our work.

Anna and I continued developing this protocol. We published a training manual and workbook, and in 1998 began the two-day Certified Compassion Fatigue Specialist Training (CCFST) at the Traumatology Institute. This training taught other clinicians to utilize the ARP in their practice for working with professional caregivers and service providers who were suffering symptoms related to their work. This training was highly successful, and we began to offer it around the country. As I began to treat a growing number of professionals with the ARP and facilitate the CCFST, I made a very interesting discovery. While the ARP was designed to simply ameliorate work-related symptoms, what I was discovering was that the folks who completed the treatment protocol and participants who took the two-day training were not only reporting a lessening of symptoms, they were also articulating that they had undergone a complete professional (and frequently personal) transformation. They described their work becoming fun and rewarding again. They emailed and said that their personal relationships had deepened and become much more satisfying following the completion ofthe treatment or workshop. While we had set out to simply create a treatment process for those suffering from work-related symptoms, what we soon found was that we had stumbled upon a catalyst for transformation. This early work has shaped everything I now do with the treatment of trauma.

In 1999, after witnessing these profound changes with workshop participants and those who completed the ARP, we began collecting data and found that, indeed, the workshop was an effective treatment for the symptoms of compassion fatigue. Our early publications (2000; 2002) detail the training-as-treatment effect that has become the hallmark of our compassion fatigue trainings. To date, there have been eleven published peer-reviewed articles that demonstrate the positive treatment effects of our trainings—including the one in which you are participating.

Buoyed by all of this positive and interesting data, Anna and I decided to try to work on the front end of compassion fatigue. We mused: If the ARP was an effective treatment for compassion fatigue and the training in these skills was lessening symptoms for the participants, could these principles and protocols prevent compassion fatigue symptoms? This was the impetus for the development of the one-day Compassion Fatigue Prevention training (as it was originally titled in 1999/2000). In 2004, 2005, and 2009 we published articles demonstrating the prevention capacity of this one-day workshop, now called the Professional Resilience and Optimization workshop. The 2004 study, with animal care professionals, was particularly exciting because we were able to demonstrate a significant lessening of Trait Anxiety on the STAI after the training and then another significant lessening of the measure of characterological anxiety (that is supposed to remain constant through a person's life) after an eighteen-month follow-up.

Over the past twenty years, we have treated hundreds and trained tens of thousands of care professionals and volunteers to be heartier, healthier, and less symptomatic in pursuit of their mission of serving the suffering and traumatized. We have had the good fortune of being catalysts for transformations in the professional and personal lives of these heroes. I am humbled and grateful to have been chosen as one of the stewards of this powerful and potent collection of principles and practices of professional resilience and maturation.

We are excited that you have chosen to join us on this voyage into developing professional and personal resilience. We hope you are one of the people who experience this transformative process and find your passion for your work rekindled as you go forward with lessened work-related symptoms.

You are the reason that we do what we do. We look forward to hearing about how this process has impacted you. More than anything else, we want you to know that now, in the twenty-first century, you do not have to suffer to provide good care to your patients and clients. If you are suffering from your work, you are doing it wrong! We also want you to know that we are here for you. If you find yourself suffering from your work anytime in the future and you are ready to do something about it, then contact us. You have my solemn word that we will help you find the resources that you need.

It's Simple, but NOT Easy

This course offers tangible skills that you can implement immediately in your personal and professional life. Once you learn these skills, you will know how to never experience stress again. These skills are simple. They do, however, require discipline, intention, and ongoing commitment to gain benefit from them.

This workshop and workbook offer a disciplined way of moving through your professional (and personal) world. They provide knowledge about what happens to our bodies when we perceive threats and will teach you how to intentionally regulate this autonomic process so that you are no longer generating symptoms and suffering from your work and life. As you develop and master these skills, you will find that you are able to become more intentional—more principle-based and aligned with your own integrity—in both personal and professional realms. One constant we have discovered throughout this work is that no one is willing to embark upon the challenging journey of developing, practicing, and mastering the skills until they have suffered enough from not doing so. Have you?

It's Not Your Environment

Professional caregivers work in a variety of different and often difficult environments. Sometimes we feel we lack the money, time, or support we believe we need in order to perform optimally in our jobs. This can feel stressful. It's normal to think the high demands of our work or the lack of a supportive environment are causing compassion fatigue and burnout. This course will demonstrate to you that it is not the environment that is creating these feelings of stress. It is, instead, what is happening in our bodies while encountering these situations. And these physiological processes—stemming from your perceptions of the environment—can be intentionally interrupted and regulated. After completing this course, you will be able to work in difficult environments with difficult people and remain stress free.

It's More Than Self-Care

Taking care of ourselves is essential, but it is only one (small) component of professional resilience. It is important to take vacations, eat right, exercise, and engage in activities that bring us joy, but prevention and treatment of compassion fatigue and its companions involves much more than a good self-care plan. This training and manual provide the knowledge and skills to lessen the symptoms of compassion fatigue so that you can live with your work-related symptoms reduced to a level of comfort. Self-care is the fuel that allows you to continue forward into situations of high demand. This course teaches how to navigate those situations without becoming diminished or symptomatic.

Caregiving Affects All of Us

You have chosen this career and/or these tasks of caregiving. We respect you for making that choice. You are our brothers and sisters in this mission. Because you have chosen this path and go to work every day—even when you don't feel like it—people are alive today, in pursuit of their dreams, and enjoying a better quality of life because you were there for them in some way. We honor, value, and respect your commitment and dedication to serving the needs of others who are traumatized, suffering, or less fortunate. Our guild or fellowship of care providers is the world's immune system, helping to heal, grow, and evolve humankind. This is a noble purpose.

While most of us love our work, it is not without its challenges. Even though we enjoy high levels of satisfaction, it does not exempt us from the painful parts of giving care to others. There is no way to do this work without it hurting, but, seemingly paradoxically, you do not have to suffer (we will unpack this paradox throughout the course and this workbook). We want to invite you to embrace the understanding that you have chosen this life path. Many of you paid thousands of dollars to train for this work; many of you competed for the positions you now fill. You are not victims of your work! We will be asking you to relinquish, or "cash in," the dubious secondary gains you may receive from perceiving yourself as a victim of your caregiving work. Holding this perception that our work is the cause of our distress is an external locus of control and victimizes us. During this course, you will learn that it is what is going on inside of you while you are encountering the myriad contexts and circumstances in your work—not the contexts and circumstances themselves—that causes your work-related symptoms. It is transformational when professional and volunteer care providers "get" this, because it begins a new pathway where we have traction and can see things immediately get better for us.

Let's begin ...

Book I:
The Problem

Activity: Silent Witness

Step 1: In the space below, write down three ways you have been negatively affected by the work you do.

1.

2.

3.

Step 2: Silently share what you wrote with at least one companion. Hold up your workbook so that others can read what you wrote, and they will do the same. As you read what others wrote, you are welcome to nod your head in acknowledgment and validation. Please keep verbal responses to a minimum.

Step 3: Discuss the answers to the following questions:

- What did you notice happening in your body as you were witnessing others' symptoms and displaying your own?
- What were you thinking as you were witnessing others' symptoms and displaying your own?
- Did these feelings and thoughts change as you were witnessing others' symptoms and displaying your own?

You Are Not Alone!

All caregivers experience negative effects from their work. It's impossible not to be impacted by the individuals we work with. How do you sit with someone who is dying or who has just been raped and not be impacted by those stories and experiences?

Many of the ways in which our work negatively impacts us are universal—we get angry. We get fatigued. We lose sleep. We work harder. We work less. Yet, we rarely talk openly about them or acknowledge them.

Being able to share openly, honestly, and vulnerably with a small cadre of peers in our support network is a powerful tool for lessening work-related symptoms. These effects have been documented in many recent research studies. We simply have to develop support—giving and receiving—if we want to have longevity as care providers.

Viktor Frankl's Cornerstone

Viktor Frankl (1905–1997) was a neurologist/psychiatrist in Vienna, Austria. He was married to Tilly Grossman in 1941. On September 25, 1942, Frankl, his wife, and his parents were deported to the Nazi Theresienstadt ghetto/concentration camp. On October 19, 1944, Frankl and his wife Tilly were transported to the Auschwitz concentration camp, where he was processed. He was moved to Kaufering, a camp affiliated with Dachau, later that October, where he spent five months working as a slave laborer. In March 1945, he was offered a move to the so-called rest camp Türkheim, also affiliated with Dachau, where he worked as a physician until April 27, 1945, when the camp was liberated by American soldiers.

During his years of internment in the Nazi death camps, Dr. Frankl underwent a powerful transformation that has reverberated through and helped evolve humankind for the past seventy years. While he was tortured, starved, without clothing, and utterly bereft, he found hope. He also found joy. He found peace. He found purpose and meaning. And, according to him, he found the greatest of gifts that life has to offer—he found love. In a Nazi death camp!

He writes about this in *Man's Search for Meaning*:

> We stumbled on in the darkness, over big stones and through large puddles, along the one road leading from the camp. The accompanying guards kept shouting at us and driving us with the butts of their rifles. Anyone with very sore feet supported himself on his neighbor's arm. Hardly a word was spoken; the icy wind did not encourage talk. Hiding his mouth behind his upturned collar, the man marching next to me whispered suddenly: "If our wives could see us now! I do hope they are better off in their camps and don't know what is happening to us."

> That brought thoughts of my own wife to mind. And as we stumbled on for miles, slipping on icy spots, supporting each other time and again, dragging one another up and onward, nothing was said, but we both knew: each of us was thinking of his wife. Occasionally I looked at the sky, where the stars were fading and the pink light of the morning was beginning to spread behind a dark bank of clouds. But my mind clung to my wife's image, imagining it with an uncanny acuteness. I heard her answering me, saw her smile, her frank and encouraging look. Real or not, her look was then more luminous than the sun which was beginning to rise.

A thought transfixed me: for the first time in my life I saw the truth as it is set into song by so many poets, proclaimed as the final wisdom by so many thinkers. The truth—that love is the ultimate and the highest goal to which Man can aspire. Then I grasped the meaning of the greatest secret that human poetry and human thought and belief have to impart: The salvation of Man is through love and in love. I understood how a man who has nothing left in this world still may know bliss, be it only for a brief moment, in the contemplation of his beloved. In a position of utter desolation, when Man cannot express himself in positive action, when his only achievement may consist in enduring his sufferings in the right way—an honorable way—in such a position Man can, through loving contemplation of the image he carries of his beloved, achieve fulfillment. For the first time in my life I was able to understand the meaning of the words, "The angels are lost in perpetual contemplation of an infinite glory."

Dr. Frankl was able to develop and sustain quality of life while enduring the infinite horror and squalor of existence in some of the worst circumstances ever endured by humankind. His adaptation and resilience are legendary. He chronicled these experiences in *Man's Search for Meaning* and left us with a powerful legacy: Our quality of life need not be determined by our external context.

Understanding, embodying, and promulgating this truth, as a care provider who has routinely sat across from thousands of survivors of trauma for the past thirty-five years, has been one of the most important professional development leaps of my career. Viktor Frankl's gift to me was the ability to make my hope—for my clients and myself and for all of humankind—incandescent. My hope no longer diminishes when I sit across from someone who has lost everything, because I now know that no matter how bad the circumstances, anyone can find joy, peace, purpose, meaning, and love in those circumstances. I will forever be in debt to Dr. Frankl, both professionally and personally. It is my hope to embody and carry on a little bit of his legacy as I go forward in my career.

After Dr. Frankl was liberated from the Nazis, he went on to spend the next fifty-plus years of his life continuing to be of service to those who suffered and were traumatized. I believe he earned the right to make some pronouncements about what is required to become a resilient care professional, and those of us studying and trying to create resilience and quality of life for others ought to pay heed to his lessons. One of his many pithy quotes provides a deeper understanding of what is required to thrive as a care professional.

What is to give light must endure burning.

In this quote from *Man's Search for Meaning*, Dr. Frankl established the cornerstone of our work with compassion fatigue. It contains both a warning and a prescription. The warning is this: Those of us who have dedicated our lives to the service of others, who share a mission of helping and healing, who have chosen to give light— we are going to burn. It is inevitable. There is no way to empathetically witness pain and suffering in others without it also causing us pain. Recent brain research has confirmed this truism. There is no navigation through a career of caregiving that does not force caregivers to confront heartbreak, loss, bewilderment, horror, frustration, rage, and having our most sacred beliefs shaken. Some have learned to turn off their empathy and become numb to the pain of others as they limp through their work with their sights set only on the completion—of their day, until vacation, until retirement, until they die. Others simply leave the field, abandon their mission, and find some degree of solace in work that is much less emotionally and spiritually demanding. A precious few grow resilience. They learn what, I believe, Viktor Frankl was trying to tell us in that quote: that while pain is inevitable and acute, it need not metastasize into chronic suffering.

As we grow the capacity to tolerate and even embrace the pain of our work, instead of avoiding or fighting it, we begin to find beauty, indomitability, and heroism in clients and in ourselves. I believe this alternative is what Dr. Frankl discovered in a Nazi death camp, and I am certain this completely different reality of sustainable confrontation of pain without suffering is available to us all. I am deeply grateful to Dr. Frankl for forging this pathway that I hope we have widened a little in our work with compassion fatigue. We would like to invite you down this pathway with us during this workshop.

Hippocrates and the Myth of Stoicism/Objectivity

Dr. Frankl's perceptual shift stands in stark contrast to what many of were taught, either explicitly in our training programs or implicitly through our encounters with other professionals early in our careers. Many of us learned what Hippocrates taught his medical students at the Lyceum in early Grecian civilization. Hippocrates, the father of medicine, taught that if the physician was able to remain stoic enough and vigilantly objective with his patients, then he would not contract the suffering from those patients. He intimated that this applied to both the physical illnesses and the spiritual/emotional maladies.

This perception has been a blight on the field of medicine for 2,500 years. As the field of mental health, born from psychiatry, began to formally develop a century or so ago, this paradigm was already firmly established. Most of us were taught (by academics who did not spend their careers witnessing this suffering) or unconsciously believe that there is some mystical pathway through caregiving work that does not hurt the care provider. If we just suck it up and become more hardened, we will be fine. Work-related stress symptoms, viewed through the lens of this paradigm, are a sign of weakness. As we begin to find that we are hurting from our work, the only meaning available to us to make sense of this is that there must be something wrong with us. We compare our insides with our peers' outsides. In this one-dimensional view, it looks like others have figured this out and they are not carrying pain in their work like we are. We begin to believe that everyone else can do this work without it being so painfully difficult. And this may be the most insidious symptom associated with compassion fatigue. Stuck in this perceptual quagmire, we are forced to hide from our peers and be at war with ourselves. We are unable to share honestly with the people who are available to support us, for fear they will discover that we are inadequate, fraudulent, and unequipped to be in our position of helping others. We become increasingly isolated, eschewing genuine connection in favor of defense and minimizing discomfort.

This method of coping is unsustainable. All care providers, even the most technical neurosurgeons or nuclear medicine engineers, require relationships with patients, peers, administrators, support staff, and ourselves to sustain and enjoy a career in caregiving. When meaningful relationships are truncated, the suffering caregiver frequently turns to external agents and processes to soothe their discomfort. They drink a little more alcohol, they take drugs (illicit or prescribed), they over- or under-eat, they compulsively watch television, they act out sexually, they over-spend, or any combination of self-destructive methods of coping. The diminishing returns of self-destruction as a lifestyle ultimately lead the practitioner to crisis. This may be a health crisis, a divorce, an arrest, emergence of mental illness, getting reprimanded or fired, or some other life circumstance that demands our attention and demands that we change the way we are living. This is how most of the people I have treated for compassion fatigue have found their way to me. It took a crisis to shake them awake from their semi-conscious lives and help them choose to make real change toward a better, more fulfilling life.

Hopefully, during the Silent Witness exercise and discussion, you gained a little insight into these processes. We hope you are leaving today's training with a few of these insights:

1. We are ALL affected by our caregiving work. No one does helping work without some kind of impact. As Henri Nouwen taught us in 1969, we are all Wounded Healers. You are not alone, and chances are, you can reach out to some of your colleagues and peers to share some of your experiences and get some professional and social support.

2. Most people cope with the symptoms of compassion fatigue through suppression, avoidance, and denial of these symptoms. This is not an effective coping strategy for managing work-related stress. Unaddressed compassion fatigue always gets worse and, like alcoholics, we do not start getting better until we admit that there is a problem.

3. Compassion fatigue is a downward progression, and as the symptoms get worse, our ways of coping often become more desperate until they reach a crisis point. Hopefully, you now understand that you do not have to wait for things to get worse before they get better. We invite you to fully participate in this workshop—in practicing the skills contained in this workbook—and begin your journey toward resilience and optimization. The first step of a journey is the most important step, because it heralds the direction in which you are traveling.

Did You Know?

Hippocrates developed an oath that reflected his medical ethical views. Today this oath is known as the Hippocratic Oath and is taken by newly qualified doctors as a pledge of ethical behavior towards patients—evidence of Hippocrates' continuing influence on medicine today.

How Compassion Fatigue Impacts Us

Researchers have identified a set of symptoms that are associated commonly with compassion fatigue. Are your negative effects from your job listed here? Check the ones that apply to you.

Physical Symptoms

❑ I have had increased absenteeism or "sick days"
❑ I have been feeling physically ill
❑ I have been feeling fatigued
❑ I have been feeling keyed-up and nervous
❑ I am doing less rather than more exercise
❑ Normal sleep has been more difficult for me
❑ I have lost enjoyment in intimate and sexual activities

Psychological Symptoms

❑ I have noticed myself being more cynical and pessimistic
❑ I have noticed myself trying to avoid feelings by numbing or shutting down
❑ I have had work-related nightmares/bad dreams
❑ I have lost interest and enjoyment in activities
❑ I have difficulty in making decisions or make poor decisions
❑ I feel like I have lost some of my self-esteem

Emotional Symptoms

❑ I have anger directed toward my supervisors or co-workers
❑ I have been feeling flat, depressed, and hopeless more than I used to
❑ I have been more angry and irritable than normal
❑ I have moments of dread when thinking about going to work
❑ I am having trouble finding hope
❑ I am less connected to my spiritual and religious beliefs than I used to be
❑ I have felt overwhelmed more than three times in the past week

Spiritual Symptoms

- ❏ I have been avoiding spending time with my friends and family
- ❏ I fear for the safety of myself and my loved ones
- ❏ I have engaged less rather than more in activities that used to bring me pleasure
- ❏ I have had a lack of time for self
- ❏ I find it difficult to trust others
- ❏ I have feelings of despair and hopelessness

Professional Symptoms

- ❏ I have been unable to get work or something specific to work out of my head
- ❏ I have had unwanted memories pop up in my head of past events from work
- ❏ My productivity at work has been reduced
- ❏ I have felt like quitting my job more than once
- ❏ I find paperwork and menial tasks getting in the way of my enjoyment of work

Note: Five or more checked could indicate that you are suffering from compassion fatigue.

Symptoms of Secondary Traumatic Stress

Intrusive Symptoms

Thoughts and images associated with patients' traumatic experiences and/or sufferi[ng]

Obsessive and compulsive desire to help certain patients

Patient/work issues encroaching upon personal time

Inability o "let go" of work-related matters

Perception of patients as fragile and needing the assistance of caregiver ("savior")

Thoughts and feelings of inadequacy as a care provider

Sense of entitlement or specialness

Perception of the world in terms of victims and perpetrators

Personal activities interrupted by work-related issues

Avoidance Symptoms

Silencing response (avoiding hearing/witnessing client's traumatic material)

Loss of enjoyment in activities/cessation of self-care activities

Loss of energy

Loss of hope/sense of dread working with certain patients

Loss of sense of competence/potency

Isolation

Secretive self-medication/addiction (alcohol, drugs, work, sex, food, spending, etc.)

Relational difficulties

Arousal Symptoms

Increased anxiety

Impulsivity/reactivity

Increased perception of demand/threat (in both job and environment)

Increased frustration/anger

Sleep disturbance

Difficulty concentrating

Change in weight/appetite

Somatic symptoms

Compassion Fatigue and Ethics Violations

Research has shown that as compassion fatigue and secondary traumatic stress increase, so do ethical breaches in professional standards. Those who behave unethically in their jobs are making decisions with their autonomic nervous system activated, which turns off logical thinking centers and impulse control. No wonder those who behave unethically often say, "I don't know what I was thinking!" They weren't thinking!

Self-Assessment: How Do You Know If You Have Compassion Fatigue?

In 1993, researcher Beth Stamm created the Professional Quality of Life Scale (ProQOL) to measure compassion satisfaction, burnout, and secondary traumatic stress. The ProQOL is the gold-standard measure of work-related stress. We recommend using the ProQOL at least once a year to be aware of your compassion fatigue and stress levels and be proactive in addressing them. Since we all experience negative effects from our work, the ProQOL should not be used at work to predict job performance.

On the next page you will find a copy of the ProQOL-5. We recommend you complete this self-assessment instrument. Then, using the following pages, score the instrument on its three subscales—compassion satisfaction, secondary traumatic stress, and burnout. Having completed this instrument before the workshop will better prepare you for the material during the workshop.

Professional Quality of Life Scale (ProQOL)

Compassion Satisfaction and Compassion Fatigue (ProQOL) Version 5 (2009)

When you help people, you have direct contact with their lives. As you may have found, your compassion for those you help can affect you in positive and negative ways. Below are some questions about your experiences, both positive and negative, as a helper. Consider each of the following questions about you and your current work situation. Select the number that honestly reflects how frequently you experienced these things in the last thirty days.

1=Never   2=Rarely   3=Sometimes   4=Often   5=Very Often

1._____I am happy.

2._____I am preoccupied with more than one person I [help].

3._____I get satisfaction from being able to [help] people.

4._____I feel connected to others.

5._____I jump or am startled by unexpected sounds.

6._____I feel invigorated after working with those I [help].

7._____I find it difficult to separate my personal life from my life as a [helper].

8._____I am not as productive at work because I am losing sleep over traumatic experiences of a person I [help].

9._____I think that I might have been affected by the traumatic stress of those I [help].

10._____I feel trapped by my job as a [helper].

11._____Because of my [helping], I have felt "on edge" about various things.

12._____I like my work as a [helper].

13._____I feel depressed because of the traumatic experiences of the people I [help].

14._____I feel as though I am experiencing the trauma of someone I have [helped].

15._____I have beliefs that sustain me.

16._____I am pleased with how I am able to keep up with [helping] techniques and protocols.

17._____I am the person I always wanted to be.

18._____My work makes me feel satisfied.

19._____I feel worn out because of my work as a [helper].

20._____I have happy thoughts and feelings about those I [help] and how I could help them.

21._____I feel overwhelmed because my case [work] load seems endless.

22._____I believe I can make a difference through my work.

23._____I avoid certain activities or situations because they remind me of frightening experiences of the people I [help].

24._____I am proud of what I can do to [help].

25._____As a result of my [helping], I have intrusive, frightening thoughts.

26._____I feel "bogged down" by the system.

27._____I have thoughts that I am a "success" as a [helper].

28._____I can't recall important parts of my work with trauma victims.

29._____I am a very caring person.

30._____I am happy that I chose to do this work.

What Is My Score and What Does It Mean?

In this section, you will score your test so you understand the interpretation for you. To find your score on each section, total the questions listed on the left and then find your score in the table on the right of the section.

Compassion Satisfaction Scale

Copy your rating on each of these questions here and add them up. When you have added them up, you can find your score on the table to the right.

3. _____
6. _____
12. _____
16. _____
18. _____
20. _____
22. _____
24. _____
27. _____
30. _____

Total: _____

The sum of my Compassion Satisfaction questions is	So my score equals	And my Compassion Satisfaction level is
22 or less	43 or less	Low
Between 23 and 41	Around 50	Average
42 or more	57 or more	High

Why Measure Compassion Satisfaction?

The ProQOL measures compassion satisfaction because the more compassion satisfaction you have, the more resilient you are. Resilience allows us to work in challenging environments without having negative effects. A high score in this area is ideal and can neutralize burnout and secondary traumatic stress.

Burnout Scale

On the burnout scale you will need to take an extra step. Starred items are "reverse scored." If you scored the item 1, write a 5 beside it. The reason we ask you to reverse the scores is because scientifically the measure works better when these questions are asked in a positive way, though they can tell us more about their negative form. For example, question 1, "I am happy," tells us more about the effects of helping when you are **not** happy, so you reverse the score.

*1. _____ = _____

*4. _____ = _____

8. _____

10. _____

*15. _____ = _____

*17. _____ = _____

19. _____

21. _____

26. _____

*29. _____ = _____

Total: _____

The sum of my Burnout questions is	So my score equals	And my Burnout level is
22 or less	43 or less	Low
Between 23 and 41	Around 50	Average
42 or more	57 or more	High

Secondary Traumatic Stress Scale

Just like you did on Compassion Satisfaction, copy your rating on each of these questions and add them up. When you have added them up, you can find your score on the table to the right.

2. _____

5. _____

7. _____

9. _____

11. _____

13. _____

14. _____

23. _____

25. _____

28. _____

Total: _____

The sum of my Secondary Traumatic Stress questions is	So my score equals	And my Secondary Traumatic Stress level is
22 or less	43 or less	Low
Between 23 and 41	Around 50	Average
42 or more	57 or more	High

Your Scores on the ProQOL: Professional Quality of Life Screening

Based on your responses, place your personal scores on the next two pages.

Compassion Satisfaction _____

Compassion satisfaction is about the pleasure you derive from being able to

do your work well. For example, you may feel like it is a pleasure to help others through your work. You may feel positively about your colleagues or your ability to contribute to the work setting or even the greater good of society. Higher scores on this scale represent a greater satisfaction related to your ability to be an effective caregiver in your job.

The average score is 50 (SD 10; alpha scale reliability .88). About 25% of people score higher than 57 and about 25% of people score below 43. If you are in the higher range, you probably derive a good deal of professional satisfaction from your position. If your scores are below 40, you may either find problems with your job, or there may be some other reason—for example, you might derive your satisfaction from activities other than your job.

Burnout _____

Most people have an intuitive idea of what burnout is. From the research

perspective, burnout is one of the elements of Compassion Fatigue (CF). It is associated with feelings of hopelessness and difficulties in dealing with work or in doing your job effectively. These negative feelings usually have a gradual onset. They can reflect the feeling that your efforts make no difference, or they can be associated with a very high workload or a non-supportive work environment. Higher scores on this scale mean that you are at higher risk for burnout.

The average score on the burnout scale is 50 (SD 10; alpha scale reliability .75). About 25% of people score above 57 and about 25% of people score below 43. If your score is below 43, this probably reflects positive feelings about your ability to be effective in your work. If you score above 57, you may wish to think about what at work makes you feel like you are not effective in your position. Your score may reflect your mood; perhaps you were having a bad day or are in need of some time off. If the high score persists or if it is reflective of other worries, it may be a cause for concern.

Secondary Traumatic Stress _____

The second component of Compassion Fatigue (CF) is secondary traumatic stress (STS). It is about your work-related, secondary exposure to extremely or traumatically stressful events. Developing problems from exposure to others' trauma is somewhat rare, but does happen to many people who care for those who have experienced extremely or traumatically stressful events. For example, you may repeatedly hear stories about the traumatic things that happen to other people, commonly called vicarious traumatization. If your work puts you directly in the path of danger, for example, field work in a war or area of civil violence, this is not secondary exposure; your exposure is primary. However, if you are exposed to others' traumatic events as a result of your work, for example, as a therapist or an emergency worker, this is secondary exposure. The symptoms of STS are usually rapid in onset and associated with a particular event. They may include being afraid, having difficulty sleeping, having images of the upsetting event pop into your mind, or avoiding things that remind you of the event.

The average score on this scale is 50 (SD 10; alpha scale reliability .81). About 25% of people score below 43 and about 25% of people score above 57. If your score is above 57, you may want to take some time to think about what at work may be frightening to you or if there is some other reason for the elevated score. While higher scores do not mean that you do have a problem, they are an indication that you may want to examine how you feel about your work and your work environment. You may wish to discuss this with your supervisor, a colleague, or a health care professional.

What Do Your Scores Tell You?

Use the space below to write a few thoughts about your scores on the ProQOL. Were your scores what you expected? Why or why not?

_____

_____

_____

_____

_____

_____

Step 1: In the space below, write down three things you do really well while performing your job. If there are more than three, write as many as you can!

_____

_____

_____

_____

Step 2: Answer these questions in the space below. Is your job stressful? If so, what is it about your workplace that makes it stressful? What are some of the ways you see stress affecting your coworkers?

_____

_____

_____

_____

Step 3: Answer these questions in the space below. What are some of the things that make this work valuable? Why do you do it?

_____

_____

_____

_____

Step 4: Share your answers with someone else and include a verbal answer to this question: Are the rewards of your job enough to compensate for the stress you experience?

Notes:

Tools for Hope

Perceived Threat, the Autonomic Nervous System, Self-Regulation, and Intentionality

Education   *Identity*   *Activity*   *Sharing*

Engagement

Would you be interested in learning, over the next thirty minutes, how to eradicate stress from your life?

"Yeah, right." Most of us cannot hear this statement without a little skepticism; however, it is equally difficult to resist the temptation to hear how we might manage this seemingly impossible task. Even the most recalcitrant clients can muster enough willingness and open-mindedness to listen, albeit skeptically, for the next half-hour. In individual treatment, this is where we ask our clients to identify the sources of stress, or stressors, they perceive in their lives. Most clients recite a litany of objects, people, and activities they believe to be the causes of their stress. These might include things like finances, relationships, work, traffic, the economy, etc. Following the creation of this list of "causes," the therapist can now elicit the "effects" of stress from their client: What effects are all these stressors having in your life?

The answer to this question is usually a summary list of the symptoms for which the client has sought treatment. Somatic problems (e.g., headaches, GI disturbances, chronic pain, etc.), anger/irritability, sleep problems, over-/under-eating, substance abuse, relational problems, and anxiety are the more commonly reported effects of these stressors.

Causes and Effects of Stress

Causes
Work
Finances
Health Concerns
Relationships
Aging
Children
Politics
Demands

Effects
Anxiety
Depression
Irritability
Fatigue
Sleep Problems
Over-/Under-Eating
Isolation
Somatization

This next step in using this process therapeutically is precarious and needs to be offered with equal parts compassion and humor. The clinician holds up these two lists and, pointing to the list of "causes," says:

These are NOT the causes of your stress. As long as you believe that these ARE the causes of your stress, there is a good chance you will keep having these (pointing now at the list of "effects").

Occasionally, clients may become a little irritated with this confrontation, and the clinician will need to assure them that they have offered this with compassion and ask for permission to continue to pursue the REAL cause of their stress. Most clients, by this point, are very much engaged and interested in what is coming next.

Continuing, the next important step is to reveal the true cause of stress. That is: STRESS = PERCEIVED THREAT. Perceived threat is the single cause of all stress in human beings. We experience stress when we encounter financial or relational difficulties, or at work, or in traffic, because we have learned, through painful or fearful past experiences, to perceive threat in these circumstances. Stress is simply the body and mind's reaction to a danger. It makes no difference in our response whether this danger is real or only perceived. Perceived threat (real or imagined) activates the sympathetic nervous system, and a discussion about the changes that take place in the body and brain when the sympathetic nervous system becomes activated is the next step of this first phase of Forward-Facing Trauma Therapy (see figure below).

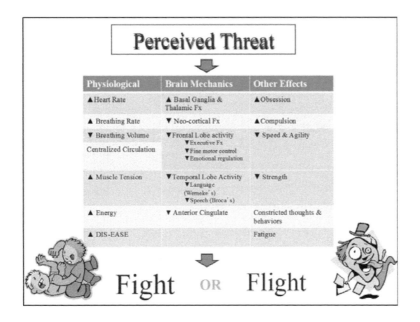

Sympathetic Nervous System

When we perceive threat, our sympathetic nervous system (SNS) activates. Only during these periods of perceived danger is the sympathetic nervous system active and, if we stay in the context of the perceived threat, the SNS will remain activated to become dominant. In medicine this is called "dysautonomia." We sometimes called it "jacked-up-ed-ness." Whatever you call it, it is a state of having too much energy in the body, producing the biofeedback of distressing symptoms. That is the purpose of stress symptoms: to let you know that you are overstimulating your autonomic nervous system—you are in the red zone. As we move through the workshop, you will learn skills of interoception to help you recognize, monitor, and intervene in this system to bring it back under intentional control. As we develop and master this capacity, we are able to not only live without stress, but optimize our cognitive and motor performance in every aspect of our lives. It is elegantly simple, but exceedingly challenging and difficult to develop this skill into mastery.

When we do not perceive threat, or when we intentionally relax our bodies, our parasympathetic nervous system (PNS) becomes and remains dominant. Parasympathetic dominance may best be described as being "comfortable in our own skin," peaceful, or content.

The physiological hallmarks of SNS dominance include increased heart and respiration rate, decreased peripheral circulation, muscle tension, and increased energy. The brain stem and basal ganglia—often referred to as the "reptilian brain"—also become more active when we perceive threat, and the neocortex, or "thinking" part of the brain, becomes recessive. Thus, the longer we spend in the context of a perceived threat without intentionally relaxing our bodies, the more we compromise the cognitive and performance areas of our brains. We become progressively less able to think clearly and rationally; more compromised in our language and memory skills; less agile and graceful; less able to creatively solve problems; and less capable of "being ourselves."

Before we impugn the SNS, however, let's look at some of the benefits of sympathetic activation (activation "good" vs. dominance "bad"). The SNS gives us energy and strength, helps us to focus, supplies excitement, and affords us with joy, anticipation, and ecstasy. It's only when the SNS gets stuck in the "on" position that it causes us problems.

How Did We Get So Anxious?

Good question. The World Health Organization recently conducted a study of personal safety in the twenty-first century, and reported that in high-income countries (North America, Europe, some of Asia, some of South America), we are the safest generation to ever live on Earth. We are less likely to become victims of warfare, pestilence, famine, disaster, crime, and several other dangers than any previous generation. With the neverending parade of trauma across the evening news, it doesn't feel very safe, though, does it? While we may indeed be the safest generation to walk the planet, we also seem to be the most afraid. We have built the safest world ever for our children … and we are scaring them to death. What separates our generation from any preceding it? Why do we perceive so much threat? That's right—the media. We bear witness to exponentially more trauma and traumatic occurrences than did any of our ancestors, through constant bombardment from the media. In 1990, Laurie Pearlman and Linda McCann, in their landmark work with vicarious traumatization, demonstrated to us that we need not be the survivor of a traumatic event to become traumatized by it—we need only witness it.

To illustrate this phenomenon, often in workshops I ask participants, "How many of you in this room have ever been attacked in a parking garage?" Usually no one raises their hand. If someone does, I ask them to sit out on answering the next question: "How many of you find yourself on-guard and anxious when you are in a parking garage?" In almost all cases, all the hands in the room go up. When I ask why they experience this anxiety, I can almost see the light bulb switch on as I hear answers like "the evening news," "*CSI*," "the newspaper," "my friend was attacked." These folks "witnessed" trauma in a parking garage, and when they later found themselves in that context, they perceived threat where there was no real danger. Add to this the phenomenon of state-dependent learning, which teaches us each and every time that we experience something painful, fearful, or uncomfortable that there is a good possibility that we will perceive future situations that remind us of this original event as threatening.

So, said differently, if a person is the survivor of a significantly traumatic experience (abuse, rape, natural disaster, motor vehicle accident, etc.), he or she is more likely to perceive generalized threat in the future. If she or he is a witness to a traumatic event, through the media, hearing stories, reading, or however that person learns about something traumatic happening to someone else, that person is likely to perceive threat and be afraid in situations similar to those witnessed.

And, finally, if we experience painful, fearful, or uncomfortable incidents in our lives, through the process of association, we are likely to perceive threat in situations that remind us of these occurrences (e.g., putting our hands on a hot

stove, receiving criticism, encountering periods of financial hardship). All these past learning experiences have the potential to cause us to perceive threat in the present when there is no danger. Again, the SNS does not care whether the threat is real or imagined; it will activate in either instance. If we stay in the context of this threat (i.e., parking garage) without intentionally relaxing our bodies, our SNS will become dominant and we will begin to experience the array of symptoms it generates (anxiety, panic, difficulty concentrating, irritability, somatic discomfort, etc.). It does not take much insight into this process before we begin to see that, for many of us, threat perception is chronic, occurring hundreds or even thousands of times each day.

The original goal of the SNS was survival—to help our ancestors recognize and rapidly respond to threats. However, over tens of thousands of years, we humans have developed a frontal lobe that has given us the capacity for reasoning and discernment. Without the capacities of a neocortex, animals must recognize and respond to every threat to their survival, since they cannot tell the difference between a real and a perceived threat. However, once we are able to discern this difference, it is no longer imperative, or even useful, to respond to perceived threat with an SNS response. There is data to support the compromise of important capacities and skills when the SNS is dominant for extended periods of time. In addition to diminished cognitive and language skills, we can also lose strength, agility, and speed. Any athlete or performance artist will confirm for you that their best performances occur when they are relaxed and PNS dominant. And any martial artist will confirm that they are better prepared to protect themselves and disable an attacker when they are also relaxed.

The Yerkes-Dodson Law

In 1908, psychologists Robert M. Yerkes and John Dillingham Dodson demonstrated the relationship between arousal and performance. This original research has evolved into the Yerkes-Dodson Law to help professionals improve performance in business, athletics, and entertainment. This law describes how optimal performance is in a curvilinear relationship with arousal. Low levels of arousal are required for good performance—no one runs quickly, plays blistering guitar solos, or successfully negotiates multi-million-dollar deals while they are napping. Measured and regulated low-level arousal is associated with optimal performance or "flow." However, once the energy in our bodies becomes dysregulated and climbs beyond optimal levels, there is a precipitous drop in performance capacities—cognitive and motor.

Not only do we experience lessened capacities when we allow the energy in our bodies to escalate without conscious regulation beyond optimal levels, we also begin to find ourselves fatigued, wrung out, and overwhelmed during and after these tasks. Recent research has illustrated this relationship a little more finely

by showing that performance capacities begin diminishing at lower levels of arousal when completing complex and challenging tasks, compared with more mundane tasks. From this research we can theorize that the more complex and challenging the task, the more we need to lessen our level of arousal. One more reason that the ability to self-regulate our own ANS, without the need of an external agent or process, is one of the primary skills for professional resilience.

The Yerkes-Dodson Curve

Optimal Performance:

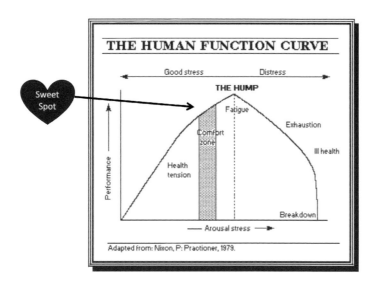

Intentionality vs. Reactivity

If we continue to perceive threat without relaxing our bodies, then our sympathetic nervous system will become and remain dominant, flooding our bodies with energy and chemicals. All that muscle-clenching, heart-racing, and shallow breathing is compelling us toward one of the two inexorable goals of the SNS—fighting or fleeing, aggression or avoidance. With the SNS dominant, we are increasingly compelled to act: to fight or fly. In this state we are progressively losing brain functioning—we are diminishing our intelligence, creativity, relational skills, coordination, stamina, and spirituality. Conversely, we are becoming more and more compelled to get out of this state. As this energy continues to ratchet upwards and our neocortical functioning continues to lessen, we will soon find ourselves acting in ways we do not want to act—compulsively and against our wills.

For example, let's say that someone criticizes you at a meeting and you perceive this criticism as a threat (later we will explore and make sense of why we perceive these threats during seemingly innocuous occurrences when we are perfectly safe).

Your face flushes, fists clench, and jaw tightens as you think of several ways to defend yourself. You decide to say nothing and allow the remark to pass, choosing to remain focused on the content of the meeting and compassionate toward your coworkers. However, you notice that you are still uncomfortable (e.g., flushed face, clenched fists, tight jaw) and progressively more irritated by the remark that occurred a few moments ago. Continuing to perseverate on the comment (therefore remaining in the context of the perceived threat), your SNS ratchets upward while, at the same time, you are losing frontal and temporal lobe functioning. Presently, while still in the meeting, you find yourself targeting angry looks and making sniping comments toward the offender (fight). After the meeting is over, you find yourself actively avoiding contact with this person for days, weeks, months, or even years (flight).

What happened? Your intention was to simply ignore the critical comment and stay true to your intention of being compassionate, tolerant, and attendant to your work. You didn't want to get drawn into these interpersonal politics, and you certainly don't want to develop and hold on to resentment, knowing that it will cause you more harm than anyone else. However, it feels as though you were powerless to stop yourself even with your best effort.

Threshold

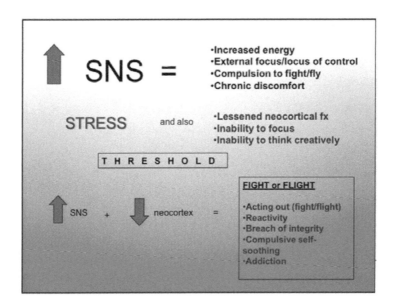

Activity

How Does Understanding Perceived Threat Help You in Your Professional or Personal Life?

Step 1: Use the space below to write a few thoughts about what you have learned so far.

_____

_____

_____

_____

_____

_____

_____

_____

Step 2: Share your thoughts with others.

Notes:

Traumagenesis: Secondary Traumatic Stress and Burnout

Education

Identity

Activity

Sharing

Compassion Fatigue

Secondary Traumatic Stress	Burnout
Cause: Witnessing/interacting with traumatized or suffering patients/clients	**Cause:** Demanding and toxic environment
	Cause Redux: Perceptions of a demanding and toxic environment
Symptoms: Nearly identcal to PTSD (intrusion + anxiety + avoidance)	**Symptoms:** Anxiety to compulsivity to hopelessness
Onset: Gradual and cumulative	
Resolution: Behavioral changes and self-regulation	**Resolution:** Perceptual change and self-regulation

Since Charles Figley first coined the phrase *compassion fatigue* in his book *Compassion Fatigue: Secondary Traumatic Stress Disorders from Treating the Traumatized*, published in 1995, several definitions and synonyms of compassion fatigue have emerged. For our purposes, we will use Professor Figley's original definition of compassion fatigue: the combined effects of secondary traumatic stress and burnout. This is also the two-factor construct that Beth Stamm has used to measure compassion fatigue symptoms with her development of the ProQOL 5.

$$CF = STS + BO$$

What Dr. Figley called secondary traumatic stress, we are going to define as all the painful learning we encounter in our lives that causes us to perceive threat from our work with traumatized, suffering, and/or demanding patients/clients. This painful learning can be experienced (i.e., a client threatening us) or witnessed (i.e., a patient telling us the story of abuse). We have called this process of past painful learning resulting in perceived threats in the present *traumagenesis*.

Burnout refers to the effects of working in a demanding, toxic, and hostile environment. These can include demanding bosses, office politics, low pay, diminishing resources, impossible demands, overwhelming schedule, technology, metrics, expectations, changing regulations, and workplace ergonomics, just to mention a few.

Even more simply stated, secondary traumatic stress is the result of our difficult and/or painful interactions with our patients/clients or their families. Burnout is the result of our interaction with our workplace environment.

Traumagenesis

All stress is traumatic stress. All the symptoms associated with stress—anxiety, irritability, compulsivity, and fatigue—are caused by painful past learning that intrudes into the individual's perception of a moment as threatening when there is no real danger. We will go into this process fully in a later chapter; however, we wanted to start here and now by introducing you to the idea that it is not the environment that is causing your stress. It is your previous painful learning sneaking into your perception of the present, resulting in the over-activation of your autonomic nervous system.

We have called this process traumagenesis. It simply means that when people have had painful learning experiences (i.e., trauma), they are likely to perceive future experiences with any sensory similarity to the original experience (e.g., the same smells, images, sounds, etc.) as dangerous. Francine Shapiro, the developer of a form of trauma treatment called Eye Movement Desensitization and Reprocessing (EMDR), has made a useful distinction between capital "T" Trauma and lowercase "t" trauma. The former is an event experienced by a person that meets Criterion A for a Posttraumatic Stress Disorder diagnosis and includes "actual or threatened death, serious injury or sexual violence." Lowercase "t" trauma includes any event that produces the perception of threat in similar contexts in the future. While not all of us have a capital "T" trauma (although recent research suggests that about 90% of Americans experience at least one of these during a lifetime), we all have hundreds, if not thousands, of lowercase "t" traumas in our lives. The result of living through all these painful learning experiences is that each time we encounter one of them in our daily lives, it makes our world perceivably a little bit more dangerous.

Take, for example, a bee sting. How many of you have ever been stung by a bee? It hurt, didn't it? Was it life-threatening? Except for the small portion of the population that has an allergic reaction to bee venom, the answer is no. However, that bee sting was a painful learning experience, was it not? Now, think about the effect that this sting (and subsequent additional bee stings) had on your perception of bees. Are you in danger when you discover a bee trapped in your car? Again, unless you are allergic, the answer is no. If you get stung it will, pardon the pun, sting, but will that sting endanger your life or limb? Nope. Think about your own physiological arousal—your stress level—when you discover that bee buzzing around in your car. What is happening to your heart rate? What are your muscles doing? What thoughts are you having? How much of your attentional focus is now upon the bee instead of driving? What compulsive behaviors do you find yourself employing (hint: fight or flight)? Do you try to kill the bee? Try to roll down the windows and shoo the bee out of the car? Do you pull over and run screaming, leaving the bee in charge of your vehicle?

Indulge us for a second more. At the risk of belaboring the point, how much danger was there to your self-being while you shared the ride with the bee? Was there a disproportionate amount of stress—much more than the context warranted? This is a good illustration of the mechanics of traumagenesis.

The bee stings of your life are all lowercase "t" traumas. However, you can see how this painful past learning quickly becomes a lens through which you perceive current sensory encounters as threatening, producing moderate to severe involuntary physiological threat responses. This perceived threat where there is little or no danger is the cause of all stress.

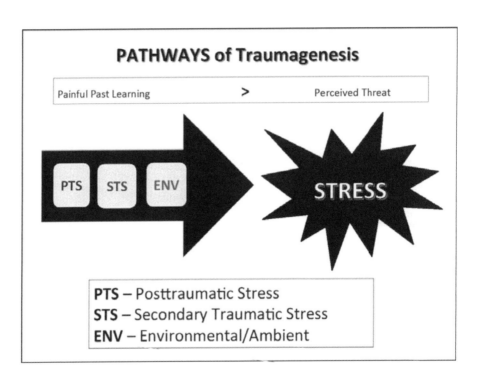

In the preceding figure, you can see that there are three ways we can become "traumatized"—or, said differently, three types of experiences that lead to the perception of threat where there is little or no danger. We have called these *posttraumatic stress*, *secondary traumatic stress*, and *environmental/ambient stress*. Posttraumatic stress refers to those encounters of painful learning that we actually experience in vivo, that we survive personally. These can be capital "T" traumas that produce PTSD and all the severe symptoms associated with that diagnosis, or they can be lowercase "t" traumas, such as the bee sting or being criticized and humiliated. We all have thousands of these experiences by the time we reach midlife. The myriad painful experiences in our past can turn our present into a jungle of perceived threats, and most of us respond instinctually with heightened arousal and brute force to navigate this jungle each day.

Secondary traumatic stress refers to those painful learning encounters that we witness but do not experience personally. These can range from watching something painful/traumatic happen to another person (i.e., a motor vehicle accident), to hearing stories (i.e., a psychotherapist listening to a patient), to witnessing physical or psychological suffering after a trauma (i.e., a nurse caring for a hospice patient), to media exposure (i.e., watching the events of 9/11 on television news). Any of these can produce the perception of threat in the present.

Activity

Step 1: Study the picture of the child in trauma below for ten seconds. As you are looking at the picture, be aware of what is happening inside of your body when you are in the context of someone who is suffering.

Step 2: Write down what you were feeling in your body. Pay attention to your muscles. What did they do?

Step 3: A picture alone is powerful enough to activate your autonomic nervous system. Discuss with a partner what you think happens when we are in the context of human suffering as part of our jobs.

How can a simple picture—albeit a provocative one—produce these physiological and psychological effects? This is the effect of secondary traumatic stress or, as McCann and Pearlman first identified it in 1990, vicarious traumatization. Their research compared the symptoms of sexual violence survivors with those of the therapists who treated them. They discovered that the therapists had the same symptoms as their clients. Since that time, there have been many studies with many different populations replicating these results. The dominant theory for why and how this happens is that when we encounter someone who has been traumatized or is suffering and we remain empathetic while engaging with or witnessing their pain, we cannot help but visualize ourselves in their position. We find ourselves "co-living" these experiences, even when they are simply stories told to us or viewed images.

A simple explanation of this is watching a movie. Think about watching a recent thriller. The music swells, the protagonist is in a life-or-death struggle with her nemesis, and you cannot turn away. You are riveted to the screen. What is happening with your heart rate? What about the muscles in your body? You don't know, do you? That is because you are completely absorbed in what you are watching, taking the sensory cues from the movie and making them your reality. You are responding as though you are in the situation in the film. If the film has a violent scene of passengers perishing in an aircraft explosion, chances are, the next time you board an airplane you will be a little more anxious about flying than you were previously.

The final pathway of traumagenesis is what we have called environmental traumatization. This is a more passive way of contracting posttraumatic stress. It is the process of becoming "infected" by others' anxiety or fear. It involves the ability of an animal, without language, to have a felt sense of danger when other animals of the same species become afraid.

In humans, children are thought to develop this capacity in utero. They are born with a felt sense of when their caregivers are anxious. This attunement, with caregivers who are mostly relaxed and able to stay focused on their child, produces a powerful bond called secure attachment. With secure attachment, children grow to become resilient and less anxious adults.

Children who grow up around anxious caregivers (and note that our species has not evolved to the level that parents can avoid this anywhere near 100% of the time with their children) spend much of their childhood watchful, afraid, and hypervigilant in the context of their anxious caregivers.

Each of us experinced this to some degree as children, and we have learned to perceive others' fear as a threat ourselves. What that means for us is that all we have to do to become traumatized is spend significant periods of time around others who are anxious, or spend large quantities of time perceiving threat without intentionally regulating the energy levels of our bodies. We frequently call this type of traumatization, especially in the professional context, burnout.

Traumatic Stress Symptoms

There are four primary groups of symptoms found in people who experience traumatic stress, according to the *Diagnostic and Statistical Manual for Mental Disorders V*:

1. Intrusion
2. Avoidance
3. Negative Alterations in Cognition and Mood
4. Arousal and Reactivity

Those with full-blown PTSD experience at least six of these symptoms, and experience them so intensely that they significantly impair functioning. Those of us who have lowercase "t" traumas, secondary trauma, or burnout still experience a wide range of these symptoms, but without reaching the threshold for the diagnosis. They can still cause high levels of distress, disrupt lives, destroy relationships, derail careers, and, at their worst, lead to passive or active self-destruction.

Intrusion	
	Nightmares about work or particular people I help
	Preoccupation with one or more of the people I help
	Perceiving the world as increasingly dangerous
	Perceiving people as victims and perpetrators
	Patient/work issues encroaching upon personal time
	Inability to "let go" of work-related matters
	Perception of patients as fragile and needing the assistance of caregiver ("savior")
	Thoughts and feelings of inadequacy as a care provider
	Sense of entitlement or specialness

Intrusion Symptoms

In PTSD, these are nightmares and flashbacks. However, with "t" traumas, secondary trauma, and burnout, this intrusive process can be as simple as perceiving threat where there is little or no danger. For example, law enforcement officers who have responded to scores of domestic disturbances where there were aggression, violence, and shifting alliances frequently report these calls as some of the most difficult of their careers. What do you suppose happens in the body and thoughts of a law enforcement officer when their radio directs them to respond to a domestic disturbance in their neighborhood? Likely dread, anxiety, expectancy of a negative experience, and hypervigilance as they knock on the door. These law enforcement officers are bracing themselves for a repeat of what they have encountered before, and that may or may not happen with this encounter.

Another subtle way that intrusive symptoms of secondary traumatic stress can affect a professional or volunteer care provider is when they become preoccupied with work or a particular patient/client. Examples of this include the nurse who calls into the unit during her off time to check on the status of a patient; the child abuse investigator who becomes angry and aggressive with all men; the woman who is caring for her mother in her home and cannot enjoy the two days of respite each month provided by an area hospice service because she is constantly concerned about her mother's health and quality of care. Each of these is a subtle way that trauma—primary or secondary, "T" or "t"—can intrude into the perceptual frame of the present, causing the care provider to perceive threat where there is no current danger.

Avoidance	
	Silencing response (avoiding hearing/witnessing client's traumatic material)
	Loss of enjoyment in activities/cessation of self-care activities
	Loss of energy
	Loss of hope/sense of dread working with certain patients
	Loss of sense of competence/potency as a caregiver
	Withdrawal and isolation
	Secretive self-medication/addiction (alcohol, drugs, work, sex, food, spending etc.)
	Relational difficulties

Avoidance Symptoms

Another way that trauma affects an individual is that they seek to avoid situations that remind them of the trauma. Avoidance could be called the "flight reaction" to threat and perceived threat in human beings. It is natural for all animals, including human beings, to avoid dangerous situations. However, people who are survivors of trauma (primary, secondary, or environmental) are also frequently compelled to avoid situations that are perceived as threatening. This is a reaction to the intrusion of painful past learning into the perception of the present. People who use avoidance as a strategy for managing their fear find themselves living ever-shrinking lives that provide few opportunities for satisfaction and mastery.

Most of us have found ourselves avoiding things that we do not want to deal with at the present moment. We have all let our mobile phones go to voicemail or made excuses to get out of a party. This is normal. However, what if the source of our pain (and therefore our fear) is work and the people we encounter at work? This includes coworkers, administrators, and even our patients and clients. What happens when this pain becomes chronic and we begin to dread going to work? It is easy to see how we can unconsciously escalate avoidance behaviors such as minimizing time with our clients, failing to engage meaningfully with our coworkers, frequent use of sick days, or working on "autopilot."

When people are chronically stressed, frequently the only way they have to cope with the dread and discomfort is to power their way through each work day so that they can "get it over with" and return. People who spend hours in this state of heightened energy and tension are suffering by the end of their day.

Negative Alterations in Cognition and Mood	
	Numbing
	Loss of hope
	Negative perspective/difficulty accessing positive mood/joyless
	Distorted perception of oneself (inadequate or superior)
	Distorted blame for symptoms (other's fault)
	Fatigue
	Loss of interest and engagement in gainful activities
	Feelings of detachment or estrangement from others

Negative Alterations in Cognition and Mood

This group of symptoms is the newest addition to the diagnosis of PTSD in the DSM-V, published in 2013. With this group of symptoms, researchers have brought forward the capacity of trauma to disrupt mood and distort perceptions of reality and oneself. Trauma impacts the brain. The more frequent and intense the past trauma of a person's life, the more likely they are to perceive threat in the present when there is little or no danger. This increased threat perception has the impact of elevating hypervigilance as a protective strategy following trauma. This chronic use of hypervigilance as a primary way of coping means that the individual is frequently compromised in their brain functioning. This can mean that their ability to perceive accurately and clearly is compromised.

The impact that this way of coping has upon perceptions of the world is that it is a chronic looming threat. As a twelve-year-old client once said, "My world has teeth." In a work context, these perceptual distortions can result in the care professional believing that the external world is the source of all their problems and distress. Workload, difficult patients, low pay, increasing demands, and co-worker politics are frequently cited as the primary causes of work-related stress. They simply are not the cause, as we will get into later in this workbook. This diminished brain functioning can also lead to distorted perceptions of oneself. Professionals exhibiting symptoms of work-related stress often have a diminished or inflated sense of self-worth. When people have a distorted sense of worth—either inflated or deflated—they are rarely, if ever, finding meaningful and restorative connection with peers and loved ones.

People who chronically perceive threat are much more likely to engage in reactive behaviors organized around trying to neutralize or avoid the perceived threat. For professional and/or volunteer caregivers who are conscripted to almost constantly engage with others, this can be exhausting. When their jobs "force" them to engage with others whom they perceive as threatening, some people cope with the perception of entrapment that comes with this loss of choice through numbing, hopelessness, resignation, and withdrawal. It is important to remember that these instinctual coping strategies are "choice-less" reactions to an overcharged autonomic nervous system and distorted perceptions of self and the world resulting from diminished brain functioning.

	Arousal and Reactivity
	Anxiety
	Irritability
	Self-destructive methods of self-soothing
	Sleep problems
	Difficulty concentrating
	Change in appetite/weight
	Somatic symptoms (headaches, GI distress)
	Feelings of detachment or estrangement from others

Arousal and Reactivity Symptoms

These symptoms are what we normally associate with distress. They are the results of a body with too much energy. Too much energy produces a physiological state of constricted muscles, elevated heart rate, change in blood chemistry, increased respiration rate, diminished blood circulation to extremities, and compromised brain functioning. All these physiological changes are not a big deal if they are momentary. However, many caregivers spend many hours of their day in a chronic state of too much energy and are experiencing these effects throughout their day. The chronicity of this state is what most of us have learned to call "stress." All these stress symptoms can be conceptualized as the body's biofeedback system telling you that you are generating too much energy. Stress symptoms are your body's dashboard letting you know you are in the red zone and running too hot.

Burnout

Do you know someone who is "burnt out"? How can you tell? We see people who are burnt out that have a darkened view of things, often pessimistic in nature. They are defensive, sharp, and critical. They gain no joy from their work anymore. They have what we like to call presenteeism: when a person is physically present, but mentally and emotionally absent. They may have difficulty connecting with clients or coworkers. If a person is still practicing while experiencing burnout, they may be engaging in malpractice due to an inability to sustain relationships. Relationships are crucial to the well-being and recovery of clients and patients. Research shows relationships are the number one reason clients heal.

Christina Maslach, a researcher on burnout, said burnout is "a syndrome of emotional exhaustion depersonalization, and reduced personal accomplishment that can occur among individuals who work with people in some capacity" (Maslach et al., 1996, p. 4). There have been other studies on burnout since 1996, and most identify the work environment as the primary cause of burnout. This mentality keeps people victims of their work. Remember, Viktor Frankl taught us it is not our environment that causes stress, but our perception of that environment. In 1998, Eric Gentry (one of the authors of this book) developed a new definition of burnout that is independent of environmental factors. Eric's definition is:

Burnout is the chronic condition of perceived demands outweighing perceived resources.

What is the operant word in that definition? Yes, *perceived*. When the real demands of life outweigh the real resources that you have to cope with these demands, you die. All other perceptions of demands and resources are distortions.

One of the most wonderful things about becoming an adult is that you no longer have any demands yoking you. You are free to choose. You get to choose everything you ever do. You have no demands upon you. You do not even have to pay taxes. You do have to accept the consequences of your choices, but you continue to make choices every moment of your life. Your job demands nothing from you.

Perhaps you, the reader, are shaking your head as you read the above couple of paragraphs. You are likely saying to yourself, "These guys don't live in the real world. If you had my life you would see just how many demands upon a person there can be." We know this because we've introduced this concept to thousands of people and their first reaction is always incredulity, if not outright hostility.

When you perceive yourself to be yoked with a demand, especially one competing with other demands that you only have a limited time to complete, what do you notice happening in your body? Think right now about your current "to-do list" and all the things you have to get done this week. What do you notice below your neck right now? If you are being honest with yourself, you will likely notice that you have some muscle constriction and budding distress as you think about all the tasks that lie in front of you this week that *need* to be accomplished. This is a tiny little microcosm of insight into what is happening with job-related stress and, ultimately, burnout. This idea will be further discussed in more detail.

We submit to you that burnout is professional learned helplessness. As long as you believe your workplace is causing you pain, the only option is to change your workplace in order to recover. How realistic is that? Most workplaces are not easy to change. We have found, however, that as you change your perceptions of your workplace, you start to shave off the toxicity of the environment. You find you are not helpless to prevent suffering deleterious effects of your job. The second part of the workbook will provide you with the solution.

Stressed?

According to a survey of the American Psychological Association, money and workplace and family responsibilities are the three major sources of stress among US adults. Levels of stress in the US vary from person to person depending on a variety of factors that can influence such feelings, including a person's employment status, age, income, and ethnicity. In 2015, it was found that millennials had the highest stress levels of any age group.

Notes:

Book II
The Solution:
Professional Maturation and
Building Your Immune System

Education

Identity

Activity

Sharing

Disease Is NOT Caused by a Toxic Environment

The Centers for Disease Control explain that illness is not caused by the presence of pathogens in the environment, but by the absence of an immune system necessary to combat these pathogens. If illness was caused simply by the presence of viruses and bacteria, we would all be ill all the time, as our environment is filled with viruses and bacteria. Instead, according to the CDC, it is the compromise of our immune systems that causes illness. Although it may seem as though many people get sick around us, only a handful do. We can remain symptom free while being exposed to pathogens if we have been inoculated or have already had the illness, because our immune system builds antibodies that protect us. We may not be able to avoid environments toxic to our mental well-being at work, but we can inoculate ourselves and develop the immunity needed to continue the work we love and are good at without becoming "ill." The "antibodies" in this case are the skills discussed in the following pages.

Resilience Skills for Enhanced Immunity

The second part of this workbook will focus on five skills essential not only for the prevention and amelioration of compassion fatigue, but for resilience and optimization in the professional caregiving environment. These are: (1) Self-Regulation; (2) Intentionality; (3) Perceptual Maturation; (4) Connection and Support; (5) Self-Care and Revitalization. Disciplined use of these skills, principles, and practices will reward the professional caregiver with greater freedom from work-related stress. Continued practice of these skills can increase your well-being in your professional and personal lives. While these skills were developed to help professionals navigate the difficult demands of the work environment, they are equally useful across all spheres of life—family, community, and personal development.

The skills for resilience and optimization offered in this workbook are born from the principles and protocols that made the Accelerated Recovery Program for Compassion Fatigue (1998; 2002; Gentry, Baranowsky, & Dunning) the first and only evidence-based treatment program for the symptoms of compassion fatigue. Over the next decade, they were researched and refined with the cooperation of health care professionals including physicians, EMTs, nurses, mental health professionals, and palliative and spiritual care professionals.

Today, the tools of this training are being utilized in many different health care contexts all over the country with clear results: professionals who practice its simple disciplines and principles find themselves happier, healthier, more productive, and less stressed. They are no longer victimized by their work or workplaces as they learn new ways of perceiving the sources of their distress and skills for ameliorating work-related symptoms.

External-to-Internal Locus of Control

All stress is traumatic stress. It is caused by the perception of threat, frequently where there is little or no real danger in the environment. However, our painful past learning intrudes into our perceptual system, causing us to see threat in a demanding patient, a client with a history of childhood abuse, or a family member navigating through end-of-life experiences. Are we in danger in any of these situations? Rarely, if ever, but when we perceive threat—real or imagined—the sympathetic nervous system activates.

This state generates the symptoms and negative effects associated with our caregiving work. We have traditionally referred to this buildup of energy as "stress." However, the concept of "stress" is usually not helpful in resolving the negative effects. It identifies outside factors as the cause of our stress, creating an external locus of control. For example, when we say, "I have a stressful job," we are saying that factors associated with our work are causing our distress AND that these factors must change in order for us to be happy, healthy, and comfortable in our work. In this way, one becomes a victim of this perception.

"My job is stressful." I have a stressful commute." "That patient always causes me stress." These are all examples of the distorted perception of stress being externally caused. The twenty-first-century understanding of perceived threat leads us to say instead, "I am constantly perceiving threat throughout the day, but I am in no danger. Let me practice relaxing my body while I encounter these perceived threats." When we do this, we are moving away from SNS dominance toward an internalized locus of control. We are more comfortable, less agitated, more intelligent, and no longer generating symptoms.

Notes:

Resilience Skill 1:
Self-Regulation

Education   *Identity*   *Activity*   *Sharing*

What Is Self-Regulation?

Self-regulation, in this context, is defined as "the intentional and conscious process of monitoring and relaxing one's body while in the context of a perceived threat, preventing the sympathetic nervous system from achieving dominance." Said more simply, self-regulation is the ability to intentionally control the activity of our autonomic nervous system (ANS). It is consistent movement away from the overstimulation of sympathetic nervous system dominance (SNS) toward the relaxed comfort of the parasympathetic nervous system (PNS), while still being engaged in activities of daily life. Said still more simply: Stop clenching the muscles in your body.

Self-regulation, as defined and employed in this treatment, is simple, but it is not easy. It involves a commitment to a lifelong practice of discovering and then relaxing constricted muscles in one's body in a disciplined and consistent way. Many people who have developed these skills find that they need to attend to their bodies in a regular and ongoing way every five minutes or so to maintain stress-free living and maximal performance. This is especially true during engagement with demanding activities. The more demanding the activity, the more we need to attend to regulating the energy in our bodies.

Relaxation vs. Self-Regulation

Self-regulation is different from relaxation, even though relaxation is a crucial part of self-regulation. We often calm our bodies by engaging in activities we consider "relaxing" to briefly escape from life. We take bubble baths, sit in hot tubs, or read fantasy novels. It's wonderful to be able to relax in such ways, but we obviously can't ask a client to wait a moment while we take a quick bubble bath to calm down because we perceive they are causing us stress. Self-regulation is not the same thing as what we often consider "relaxation." Instead, self-regulation means remaining present and actively participating in the everyday demands of work and life while we intentionally relax our body. With continued practice, we are able to modulate these systems to bring just the right amount of energy to each task, spending more of our time near optimal cognitive and motor performance as we become more proficient and disciplined in this practice. The better we become at regulating the ANS, the less fatiguing or "stressful" our work will be.

Interoception + Relaxation Response = Self-Regulation

Interoception

To introduce the concept of interoception and get an idea of how self-regulating is easy to learn but difficult to master, we are going to ask that you try this simple exercise. While sitting in a comfortable position, close your eyes and begin focusing on the sensations within your body. Scan up and down from head to toe, searching for tense muscles. Pay close attention to tension hotspots such as the jaw, neck, and shoulders.

This process of consciously shifting your attention from the outside world to the inner world of your body is what we mean when we use the medical term *interoception*, which is sometime referred to as "body-fulness." Interoception is different from mindfulness, in which we simply observe our thoughts without engaging or judging them. With interoception, our goal is to become fluent in the language of our bodies. It is the process of getting to know ourselves from the inside out, a process integral to mastering the art of self-regulation.

Many professional care providers who have successfully developed the capacity to self-regulate report that they were only able to do this after the suffering caused by work-related stress was severe enough to motivate them. They then began the process of recognizing tight muscles and simply releasing this tension—hundreds of times each day. It takes a lot of concentration to redirect our focus away from the ten thousand external happenings during a day of professional caregiving and toward the state of our physical selves. However, when we do this—when we develop this "body-fulness"—we shift from an external locus of control to one that is internal and no longer experience ourselves as victims of our environments. From this position of strength and awareness, we can become resilient, flexible, and comfortable no matter what is going on around us.

There are only two aspects of the sympathetic nervous system reaction that a person can consciously control in the midst of a perceived threat: the breath and muscle relaxation. Intentionally using your breathing and muscles to calm your body will deactivate the sympathetic nervous system reaction. Self-regulation is as simple as relaxing one's muscles while encountering the perceived threats that emerge throughout each workday. Following are some techniques to practice to begin mastering the art of self-regulation.

Self-regulation = micro-relaxation while fully engaged in life's activities.

Activity

Sample some of the methods below to find out which work best for you.

Relaxing Your Muscles (Wet Noodle)

Pay attention to how much distress and discomfort you are feeling right now. Conceptualize it on a scale of 0 to 10, with 0 being none and 10 being the most distress and discomfort you have ever felt. Think of a number.

Next, take five seconds to completely relax the muscles in your body. Pretend your muscles are like limp noodles. Let your arms and legs hang at your sides with as little tension as possible.

Evaluate how much distress and discomfort you are feeling now on a scale of 0 to 10. Did it decrease? It does. The more you are able to relax your muscles, the less distress you feel! It's that simple.

Pelvic Floor Muscles Relaxation

The vagus nerve is the largest nerve in the human body. It also happens to be one of the few two-way nerves, which means it has the ability to both receive messages from the brain and send messages to the brain. When the muscles around the vagus nerve are relaxed, the nerve sends a message to the brain telling it there is no danger and to turn off the sympathetic nervous system.

One place in the body where the vagus nerve is wrapped with muscles is in the pelvic region. When the pelvic floor muscles are relaxed, the vagus nerve signals the brain to turn off the sympathetic nervous system. Relaxing your pelvic floor muscles is one very effective way of achieving total body relaxation.

To relax these pelvic muscles, it simply takes being aware of them and thinking about relaxing them. Many people are not as familiar with these muscles, and so it takes some effort to increase awareness and relaxation. To start with, think of relaxing the muscles you would use if you were going to stop urination in midstream. Hold these muscles for five seconds and then relax them. Practice. It will be worth it.

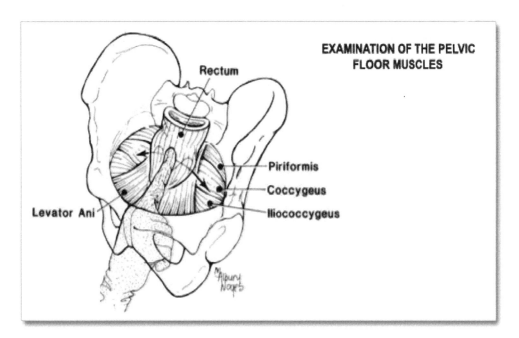

EXAMINATION OF THE PELVIC
FLOOR MUSCLES

Rectum

Piriformis

Coccygeus

Iliococcygeus

Levator Ani

Diaphragmatic Breathing

The diaphragm is a dome-shaped muscle at the bottom of your rib cage. It is used all the time for breathing. It contracts and lowers the pressure in the lungs, allowing air to enter into them. When you breathe out, the diaphragm relaxes, allowing the air to exit. As we grow older, we tend to breathe without using the power of our diaphragm, and the muscle grows weaker over time. Breathing with our diaphragm helps our body take in larger, more powerful, and deeper breaths. This sends a message to the brain that we are not in danger. Remember that the sympathetic nervous system causes our lungs to do the opposite: rapid, shallow breaths.

There are many ways to breathe with your diaphragm. One way takes only minutes to teach and even less time to master. Clasp your hands behind your head and pull your bent elbows back so they are outstretched as far as they can go in a straight line. Now breathe. You are breathing with your diaphragm. With your arms in this position, your lungs need your diaphragm to function well. As you are breathing this way, notice what happens inside your body. I hope you notice that breathing this way immediately decreases distress and discomfort throughout your body.

Peripheral Vision

The sympathetic nervous system causes our vision to narrow and hyperfocus. Activating your peripheral vision will tell your body that you are not in danger because you are no longer hyperfocused. Such a message will relax your body. To do this, focus on a spot in the room. Now continue to look straight ahead at the spot, but widen your field of vision to see how much you can notice of the room on either side of the spot. Go as wide as you can.

Activity

Step 1: Pick a dot in the middle of the picture to focus on. Stare at that dot. Expand your vision to include those around the middle dot without taking your vision off the middle dot. You will notice those dots in your peripheral vision turn black and those dots in your direct gaze remain white.

Step 2: Do this activity and notice what happens to discomfort and distress in your body.

Activity

Step 1: Identify three work situations in which you know you perceive threat and have not previously practiced any self-regulation skills—situations that "stress you out." **Example:** It's Monday morning and I'm assigned nine new patients in my already full caseload.

_____

_____

_____

Step 2: What have been the consequences of you not practicing regulating your autonomic nervous system in these contexts? **Example:** I get very sarcastic at work.

_____

_____

_____

Step 3: Discuss with a partner. Have these consequences been sufficient for you to begin the practice of self-regulation ... or do you need more severe consequences to enkindle your motivation to develop this discipline?

Activity

This activity requires a partner. The purpose of this activity is to practice moving our attention back and forth from our client/patient to our bodies, relax our body, and back again to our client. Practicing this skill will make implementing it in a client interaction much more successful.

Step 1: Turn and look into your partner's eyes for sixty seconds (you may want to set a timer). Don't say anything to each other. Just look them in the eye and stay present in the interaction. Don't let your thoughts wander to your happy place or what you have to do tomorrow. Call your attention back if it wanders. Keep checking in with your body every ten seconds and relax those muscles.

Step 2: Now decide which of you will be the sender and which will be the receiver.

Step 3: For thirty seconds, the sender will look into the eyes of the receiver with the intention of being helpful. Send all of those helpful vibes through your gaze as much as you can. The receiver's role is to allow themselves to be open to being cared for or about. In both of these roles, no verbalization is needed. You aren't doing anything but holding intention. Both the sender and receiver should keep their bodies relaxed.

After thirty seconds, switch roles and do it for another thirty seconds. Pay attention to which role (the sender or receiver) do you perceive as the most threatening. You will be able to tell this by how tight the muscles are in your body.

Step 4: Discuss with your partner. Who noticed their muscles tightening up one or more times? Were you in any danger? If not, why were you perceiving threat? Is it related to some painful past learning?

The Impact of Our ANS Dysregulation on Our Clients/Patients

What happens to our body when we are around someone who is anxious? We get more anxious. What happens when we are around someone who is relaxed? We become more relaxed. The single most important intervention we can perform as helping professionals is to be relaxed around our clients. It is important for us to be a safe place for them. We are their opportunity to heal and to repair trauma. If we are anxious, they will be too. An anxious client also loses their impulse control, logical thinking, empathy, and compassion—tools they will need to use to make good choices for themselves. Not to mention, they run the risk of being re-traumatized if they narrate a traumatic experience while in an anxious state. Keeping our bodies regulated and our sympathetic nervous systems in check ensures we have enough of a "space" that we can think clearly, logically, and intentionally. We choose our actions instead of letting our fear dictate our behavior. We can be a safe, non-anxious presence for our clients when intentionally, repeatedly practicing these self-regulation skills.

Any Threat Is a Threat:

Only 2% of threats we perceive are threats to our physical well-being. 98% of perceived threats are to our ego. Our sympathetic nervous system can't tell the difference and responds to all threats in the same way.

Notes:

Notes:

Resilience Skill 2: Intentionality

Education   *Identity*   *Activity*   *Sharing*

While self-regulation is the heart of compassion fatigue resilience, intentionality is the soul. Intentionality is about healing the moral wound of trauma.

Between Stimulus and Response there is a space.
In that space is our power to choose our response.
In our response lies our growth and our freedom.

This quote by Viktor Frankl speaks to the core importance of intentionality. At its simplest, intentionality is the ability to go where we aim ourselves. Intentionality cannot happen unless we create "space" between our sympathetic arousal due to perceived threat and our behavioral response to it. This space allows us the opportunity to act in ways congruent with our values. We are able to remain true to our core principles—both in thought and in action—while fully engaging in all of life's circumstances and contexts. Integrity is a synonym for intentionality—practicing and perfecting the art of living in alliance with one's own code or morality. Intentionality might also be articulated as being "mission-driven," or pursuing a life based upon meaning and a noble purpose. Intentionality replaces reactivity as a response to workplace and other life factors (commonly thought of as "stressors").

Think about the people you know who are suffering from stress at work—those you would call "burnt out." How reactive, impulsive, and compulsive are they? How frequently do they complain? How much do they "pop off"? How sarcastic are they? How frequently do you see them act in ways that are self-defeating and destructive? One of the consequences of being "stressed out" (i.e., SNS dominant) is reactivity—compulsive and/or impulsive behavior. When the energy created in the body by sustained SNS dominance overwhelms the neocortex's ability to manage this energy, then an individual will act out reactively. These reactive behaviors are usually regressive expressions of an attempt to neutralize the perceived threat (i.e., fight) or to get away from the perceived threat (i.e., flight). The more stressed someone is, the more likely they are to engage in reactive thinking and behaviors.

Intentionality helps us become deliberate where we were previously compulsive/impulsive or reactive. How do we create enough space to be able to intentionally choose our actions in situations of perceived threat and avoid acting in ways not congruent with our values? By using the self-regulation skills introduced previously. As we practice self-regulation in the context of workplace triggers (i.e., perceived threats), we move toward parasympathetic dominance, where we are comfortable in our bodies. As we learned earlier, in this state we have maximal neocortical functioning and are able to decide how to handle whatever present situation we encounter. This is the deliberate part of intentionality.

The integrity part involves first becoming aware of our intention. You cannot be intentional or maintain intentionality unless you are aware of what you intend. Many of us—professionals, who have gone through years of education and training in environments that demand the validation of others—have become increasingly distant from the core values that led us to pursue careers in mental health in the first place. Therefore, we start the process of intentionality by crafting our intentions into words. We have called this a covenant or personal mission statement. This statement is an articulation of the care professional's intention while at work (and in other aspects of life).

While working with helping professionals suffering from burnout, we noticed one thing they had in common was that they were in habitual breach of their integrity. A breach of integrity occurs when a caregiver acts impulsively or compulsively in the context of a perceived threat and this action is in violation of their values. Breaches of integrity occur in a multitude of ways. If you believe in treating others with kindness and respect, but then snap at the receptionist, this is a violation of your integrity. If you believe in being pleasantly responsive to your clients' needs, but you haven't responded to a voice mail message for three days, you are in breach of your integrity.

Imagine we followed you around at your job all day with a video camera. The next day, we sat together and watched the tape. In what ways would we see you breach your integrity?

Ethical Dilemmas Require Space

Working as a helping professional presents frequent ethical challenges. From deciding whether or not to accept a gift, completing paperwork properly, and navigating dual relationships, to the duty of being a mandated reporter and maintaining appropriate boundaries with clients/patients, we need all areas of our logical reasoning, memory, emotion, and impulse control working to make intentional choices. When we are in sympathetic dominance, we don't have space to be intentional with our actions. The result is that we do things we regret and are left answering the question "Why did I do that when I knew it was wrong?" Now you understand why this occurs. As a result, many professional fields have set forth codes of ethics that require a helping professional to address symptoms of stress (perceived threat) and mental well-being in order to prevent ethical breaches.

Activity

Become Aware of Your Intention

Step 1: Circle three words from the table below that articulate your purpose and/or principles at work.

Common work values and principles			
Efficient	Compassionate	Respectful	Teachable
Resilient	Healer	Helpful	Precise
Graceful	Relaxed	Tolerant	Passionate
Positive	Authentic	Fun	Thick-skinned
Focused	Thorough	Kind	Honest
Low key	Warm	Decisive	Knowledgeable
Undeterred	Team player	Leader	Articulate
Other:			

Step 2: Write those three value words in the top row of the table below.

Step 3: Identify one, two, or three situations at work where you find yourself in habitual breach of your intention to live each value. Write those situations in the table above and in the column below the value.

Activity

Become Aware of Triggers That Cause Integrity Breaches

Step 1: Looking at the table on the previous page, identify at least one trigger for each of the scenarios where you breached your integrity. Write the trigger in a box below. A trigger is something we encounter that is a perceived threat to us and causes a stress response and impulsive/compulsive thoughts and behaviors. To identify the trigger, think about what happened just before you breached your integrity.

My Triggers Table		

Step 2: Instead of brute-forcing your way through the confrontation of these triggers, can you confront them with a relaxed body? How?

_____

_____

_____

_____

Intentionality and Integrity

The integrity part involves first becoming aware of our intention. You cannot be intentional or maintain intentionality unless you are aware of what you intend. Many of us—professionals, who have gone through years of education and training in environments that demand the validation of others—have become increasingly distant from the core values that led us to pursue a career in mental health in the first place. Therefore, we start the process of intentionality by crafting our intentions into words. We have called this a covenant or personal mission statement. This statement is an articulation of the care professional's intention while at work (and in other aspects of life).

Activity

Make Your Mission Explicit

Step 1: Read the following sentences in your head and fill in the blanks with whatever pops into your head. Do this as quickly as you can.

It is my mission ...

- *To live* _____

- *To work* _____

- *To continue* _____

- *To love* _____

- *To be* _____

- *To become* _____

- *To promote* _____

- *To strive* _____

- *To seek* _____

Step 2: Answer these two questions: Why am I alive? What principles guide my behavior?

Your Mission Statement is designed to provide you with direction, purpose, and motivation toward actualizing all of your potential—professional and personal. It is written in an active and declarative voice and should empower you with a clear vision of your "best self"—the person you are becoming. This exercise is designed to help you bring into focus this "best self" and identify pathways to facilitate continued evolution toward this goal.

An Empowering Mission Statement:

1. Represents the deepest and best within you. It comes out of a solid connection to your inner life.

2. Is the fulfillment of your own unique gifts. It's the expression of your unique capacity to contribute.

3. Is transcendent. It's based on principles of contribution and purpose higher than self.

4. Addresses and integrates all four fundamental human needs and capacities. It includes fulfillment in physical, social, mental, and spiritual dimensions.

5. Is based on principles that produce quality-of-life results. Both the ends and the means are based on true north principles.
   Deals with both vision and principle-based values. It's not good enough to have values without vision—you want to be good, but you want to be good for something. On the other hand, vision without values can produce a Hitler. An empowering mission statement deals with both character and competence: what you want to be and what you want to do in your life.

6. Deals with all significant roles in your life. It represents a lifetime balance of personal, family, work, community—whatever roles are yours to fill.

7. Is written to inspire you—not impress anyone else. It communicates to you and inspires you at the most elemental level. (Covey, 1997, p.107)

Activity

Declare Your Mission

Getting your mission statement into words is important because it is a declaratio
of your intention. You are invited to make that declaration now. Refer back to the
values table, mission sentences, and questions you answered on the previous
pages to help you.

Step 1: Write a paragraph or two that summarizes your mission as a helping professiona

_____

_____

_____

_____

_____

_____

_____

_____

_____

Step 2: Share your mission statement with someone and have a discussion about how you can be intentionally living it instead of reactive.

_____

_____

_____

_____

_____

_____

_____

_____

_____

_____

_____

_____

Notes:

Resilience Skill 3: Perceptual Maturation

Education

Identity

Activity

Sharing

> *"Change the way you look at things and the things you look at change."*
>
> — Wayne W. Dyer

If we are willing to examine the ways we perceive our work and our workplace and are willing to develop a disciplined and intentional process of what we do inside of our minds, we can change our work experience. We can become excited, challenged, and stimulated instead of disheartened, overwhelmed, and stressed out. Nothing has to change in the workplace for the workplace to change. We can learn to place our attention and effort on that which we can control by regulating our physical responses and managing our thoughts. We can stop trying to manage those things that are beyond our immediate control and become more resilient, competent, and satisfied with our work.

Our work as helping professionals is stressful, right? For many of us the answer to this question is an automatic "Yes!" However, the more automatic and unconscious our "yes" response is to this question, the more likely we are experiencing negative effects from our work in the caregiving profession. There are multiple ongoing and competing demands for our time, attention, and skills. Often, these demands are more than we can accomplish with the time and resources available to us. When automatic and unexamined, they can make us increasingly uncomfortable in our work, enduring hours steeped in a "toxic" environment. Until we begin to realize that it is not the environment that causes our stress, but instead what happens inside of us as we navigate through our workday environment, we are almost certain to continue suffering the effects of stress in our professional and personal lives.

As we begin to "get it" that our stress response has an internal—not external—cause, we can start to change the way we manage our bodies and our thoughts when we encounter the multiple demands of caregiving environments. And as we move from an external to an internal locus of control, regulating our bodies and making our thoughts intentional, we find ourselves suffering less and enjoying our work more.

Once we begin to regulate our autonomic nervous systems and spend less of our time at work stressed out, we find that our brains function better. We can now move toward maturing our perception of our workplace and ourselves. Replacing our automatic and unconscious perceptions with intentional thoughts mitigates stress and enhances satisfaction in both the professional and personal arenas. The table on the next page provides a quick synopsis of each of these skills.

Choice vs Demand	• There are no demands on any of us
	• We are always "at choice"
	• Choose to do all work-related tasks, especially the undesirable ones
Acceptance of Anxious Systems/System Demands	• Acceptance that all systems demand more from us than we can give
	• You are in no danger when others want more from you than you are able to give
	• Relinquish your expectation of acknowledgement and appreciation
	• It is not your work causing you stress: it is what is happening in your body as you encounter the situations at work
Personal Best vs Outcomes	• Outcomes beyond our control
	• Aim for outcomes but focus upon present behavior
	• Do your best; it is always good enough
	• Maintain your integrity

Perceptions on Our First Day

Do you remember your first day of your first job helping others? Most of us enter the profession with what seems like an unlimited amount of energy and enthusiasm. Our perceptions often include the idea that we can save the world one person at a time, a strong sense of the importance of this work, and, if we have even considered the idea, an expectation that we will do this work without being negatively affected. Some of these beliefs were given to us by others, both in and out of the field; some we learned in school; and some stemmed from other past learning.

Somewhere along the line, most of us come to a point where every one of those beliefs we started with has been challenged. When our core beliefs about ourselves and the work are challenged, we defend them ("My perceptions can't be wrong. It must be the environment I am in."), then start to doubt ("If what I thought is wrong, maybe I'm not cut out for this work."), then search for an acceptable alternative. As a brand-new helping professional, what were your expectations, beliefs, and

perceptions about your work and yourself? As time passed, what did you come to realize about those beliefs and perceptions? How have they changed? Share these thoughts with a partner.

Unfortunately, many of us find the enthusiasm of our youthful career days dissipating as we mature in our careers. Wouldn't it be nice to have the youthful optimism and energy of our younger selves but also the wisdom and experience of our seasoned selves? In 1915, cartoonist W. E. Hill created a drawing depicting both the youthfulness of his wife and the wisdom of his mother-in-law. When you look at this picture, what do you see? Can you see both the young woman and the old woman in the picture? Most people struggle to see both figures. As a hint, the young woman's chin is the old woman's nose and the necklace on the young woman's neck is the old woman's mouth.

The Work Stays the Same; Our View of It Doesn't

This picture didn't change, but perhaps your perception of it did—as it is with our work. Multiple perceptions exist in every work environment. Just as we are learning how our ideas about "stress" can be perceived differently, we can apply those same ideas to our work, as well as to our personal lives. "Am I safe even though I don't feel safe?" may be a significant paradigm (perceptual) shift for you and for your clients.

Demand vs. Choice

Nothing is demanded of you. What is your response to this statement? What is happening in your body? Do you find yourself becoming reflexively dismissive or your muscles becoming tight? If so, this may point to the ways you have learned to perceive your workplace environment—through the experiences of your life—that can generate a significant amount of stress.

Many of us have had lifelong training—from our families, our schools, our bosses, our patients, or the media—that a request from another is a demand placed on us. The more "demands" we encounter moving throughout the workday, the more likely we are to perceive these demands as a threat and to potentially activate our sympathetic nervous system. We have covered elsewhere how this overstimulation leads to bad things (symptoms)!

To decrease the threat, we must shift from seeing work-related tasks as demands placed upon us to understanding them as activities we choose to do or not do: *I can choose to do this activity or not do this activity. What are the consequences of each decision? What is in my best interest?*

Failing to choose to engage in these activities, and understanding them instead as demands, is one of the most obvious ways in which we participate in toxifying our work environment. As soon as we perceive a request from a supervisor, a patient, or a family member as a demand, then it is most likely that we (a) will perceive that demand as a threat; (b) will have feelings of dread and avoidant behaviors associated with the demand; and (c) will likely utilize brute force (i.e., "stress") to complete the dreaded demand. We have found that choosing to engage in and complete work tasks, even the ones we don't want to do, produces significantly less stress. This simple shift in perception—"choosing"—can significantly lessen the stress you experience from your work.

Anxious Systems Demand—You Regulate

No matter how much work we do for our institutions or our patients, they are always going to demand more from us than we can give. A caregiver with an immature perception will view themselves as victimized by the fact that they can never keep up with the demands of their workplace. A caregiver with a mature perception understands that they work in an anxious system. An anxious system perceives every unserved client, every undone task as a threat to its well-being. All anxious systems are going to demand more from you than you are able to give. This is a function of the system itself, not a function of a caregiver's inability to be effective at work. Caregivers with a mature perception know that their job is to relax their body, handle each task that comes their way with integrity, and focus on the things they can control.

As we mature as professionals, we must accept this phenomenon. We must stop fighting and begin to develop the willingness and ability to (a) advocate for ourselves without polarizing with others and (b) self-regulate while working in these high-demand situations. We need to develop these skills so that we can maintain fidelity to our principles while the systems we work in try to squeeze us into breaching our integrity. This becomes a hallmark of professional resilience and maturation: Can you hold onto yourself, maintaining your principles, while your workplace demands more from you than you can give?

Outcome Driven vs. Personal Best/Principle-Based

Many of us, as caregiving professionals, allow our sense of worth to be determined by the outcomes of our work. When this happens we run the risk of developing, or exacerbating, sympathetic nervous system dominance throughout our work-day. Those who demand from themselves certain outcomes are more likely to be stressed out when some event or person negatively affects these outcomes.

A more holistic and healthy approach is to simply do the best we can in all contexts while simultaneously relinquishing the outcomes. That does not mean that we don't target treatment goals and periodically reorient our work toward these outcomes with our patients, with our colleagues/staff, and with ourselves. However, when we are in the process of actually working, we simply do our best and maintain fidelity to our principles. We can apply learning to future situations, but in the present we can only do what we can do. Paradoxically, many health care professionals report that they enjoy better outcomes when they focus on them less.

Perceptions That Promote Resilience

- There are no demands on me. I am always "at choice."
- I choose to do all work-related tasks, especially the undesirable ones, because I want to live my values, not because someone is saying I have to.
- Outcomes are beyond my control.
- I do my best and it is always good enough for today.
- My client's behavior is a feedback system for me so I can improve my quality of care.
- I will maintain my integrity.
- All systems are anxious and demand more from me than I can give.
- I am in no danger when the system wants more from me than I can give.

Relinquishing Entitlement and Secondary Gain

A common characteristic of caregiving professionals who are "burned out" is that they seem to have developed a sense of entitlement—they believe that they have sacrificed for their work and that they are owed something for this sacrifice. They have become comfortable in their victim stance, and seeing themselves as victims of their work has afforded them some secondary, albeit dubious, gains.

Every behavior gets us something, even if it is a behavior that is undesirable. While this idea may be counterintuitive, there are benefits to not changing our perceptions about our work. Has anyone ever told you, "I could never do what you do! I would not be strong enough to handle the types of cases you do and work under the conditions you do. You are a saint!"?

Many of us have heard statements like this throughout our careers. What's the message a statement like this sends?

We sometimes forget that we trained and competed to be in our current professional positions—we are NOT victims of our work. We are choosing to work where and how we do. As we become aware of the ways in which we harbor this entitlement and other secondary gains (e.g., relishing having people feel sorry for us because of the difficulty of our work), we become empowered to relinquish victimhood.

When we give up the secondary gains from suffering, we can, instead, rediscover mission and purpose in our work. Letting go of what is "owed us" allows us to rekindle the passion that made us choose this field in the first place—a desire to serve people who are hurting! As we shift away from entitlement and toward the intention of maintaining personal integrity in all our interactions (with patients, clients, coworkers, supervisors, and ourselves), work becomes a place that helps us to grow and mature, instead of a place that causes us harm. Our workplaces become places for us to practice skills that make us better people—strong, resilient, and compassionate.

Activity

Think about secondary gains you may receive from your job and how those gains are serving you. Are they serving you? Next, decide if you are willing and prepared to meet those needs in other ways. In the table below, list a few of these secondary gains and then identify alternative ways to meet those needs.

Gains from having a stressful job	Alternative plans to get it or get rid of it

Perceptions That Promote Resilience

- I am not a victim of my work. I chose and accepted the opportunity to do this work.

- I will not jeopardize my principles to get approval or worth from others.

- My work entitles me to nothing more than anyone else.

- I am conscious of the gains I am receiving from perceiving myself as victimized by my work.

- My workplace is an opportunity to practice my principles and become a better, stronger person.

Happiness

Have you ever thought, "I will be happy when . . .?" According to Shawn Achor in *The Happiness Advantage*, most of us postpone our happiness. We say things like "When I get this assignment done, I will be happy" or "When I discharge this client, I will be happy" or "When I get a raise, I will be happy."

Scientists who study happiness have found human beings tend to develop a negativity bias. A negativity bias means the brain looks for, reacts to, and stores negative information before it looks for, reacts to, and stores positive information. Therefore, if you can overcome your negativity bias and look for positive information first, you increase your chances of obtaining goals and feeling happy.

According to John Gottman, it takes at least five positive interactions to overcome a negativity bias from just one negative event. We can learn to internalize positive experiences more deeply. All kinds of good things happen to us that we hardly notice. Rick Hanson, in his book *Hardwiring Happiness*, has an activity to retrain the brain to pay more attention to positive information first.

Hanson states that we can overcome our brain's natural "negativity bias" and learn to internalize positive experiences more deeply—while minimizing the harmful physical and psychological effects of dwelling on the negative. All kinds of good things happen in our daily life that we hardly notice. We've all experienced this when someone pays us a compliment. Because of all the criticisms we've endured throughout our lives, we find ourselves dismissing or deflecting the compliment. Positive psychology seeks to help our brains learn how to tolerate and then embrace happiness by allowing ourselves a few moments to "encode" positive experiences.

Achor has developed a very practical "nuts-and-bolts" approach to achieving this "rewiring." He states:

> Realize that happiness is a work ethic. Happiness is not a mystery. You have to train your brain to be positive just like you work out your body. We not only need to work happy, we need to work at being happy. Try an experiment right now called the 21 Day Challenge. Pick one of the five habits listed on the next page and try it out for 21 days in a row to create a positive habit.
>
> 1. Write down three new things you are grateful for each day into a blank Word document or into the free app I Journal. Research shows this will significantly improve your optimism even 6 months later, and raises your success rates significantly.

2. Write for 2 minutes a day describing one positive experience you had over the past 24 hours. This is a strategy to help transform you from a task-based thinker, to a meaning based thinker who scans the world for meaning instead of endless to-dos. This dramatically increases work happiness.

3. Exercise for 10 minutes a day. This trains your brain to believe your behavior matters, which causes a cascade of success throughout the rest of the day.

4. Meditate for 2 minutes, focusing on your breath going in and out. This will help you undo the negative effects of multitasking. Research shows you get multiple tasks done faster if you do them one at a time. It also decreases stress and raises happiness.

5. Write one, quick email first thing in the morning thanking or praising a member on your team. This significantly increases your feeling of social support, which in my study at Harvard was the largest predictor of happiness for the students. (Achor, 2011, https://www.psychologytoday.com/blog/the-happiness-advantage/201108/5-ways-turn-happiness-advantage)

Resilience and happiness are closely connected. People who have the close relationships and social supports that help them during times of adversity also experience much joy and satisfaction in these relationships during everyday life. People also get feelings of pleasure and meaning from doing things well, including actions that help to overcome adversities. Happy people are not free from adversity. They are able to find meaning and purpose in their struggles, which increases satisfaction and joy.

"Owning our story can be hard but not nearly as difficult as spending our lives running from it. Embracing our vulnerabilities is risky but not nearly as dangerous as giving up on love and belonging and joy-the experiences that make us the most vulnerable. Only when we are brave enough to explore the darkness will we discover the infinate power of our light."

– Brene Brown

Vulnerability and Joy

Brene Brown is a social worker/researcher who studies what she calls "whole-hearted living," shame, and vulnerability. She studied 15,000 mental health and addiction professionals and found a connection between what gives our work purpose and meaning and vulnerability. She says those who were living "whole-heartedly" had:

1. A strong sense of love and belonging and believed they were worthy of it.
2. A sense of courage to tell their narrative openly and honestly and to be imperfect.
3. Compassion and empathy centers of the brain that were fully functioning and allowing them to show compassion to themselves.
4. Willingness to let go of who they thought they should be in order to be who they are (perceptual shifts toward authenticity)
5. Fully embraced vulnerability.

The heart of joy, peace, love, and meaning lies in our ability to be vulnerable. Vulnerability allows us to make deeper connections with our clients, coworkers, and family. We connect with them as an imperfect human being who makes mistakes because they are too. Clients, coworkers, and family feel more comfortable being authentic around us when we are not afraid to admit our vulnerabilities. We are not perceived as a threat to them. Don't be afraid to admit your mistakes and character flaws while doing this work. We aren't super human. As much as we'd like to think our clients believe we are, they know we are not. Brene Brown found that joy can not exist without vulnerability. So if you want to have joy in your work, embrace the vulnerability of it.

Fuel for Resilience

Psychologist Barbara Fredrickson and her colleagues have found that positive emotions are the fuel for resilience. Positive emotions help people find the meaning in ordinary and difficult events. Resilient people have just as many negative emotions as non-resilient people, often very intense negative emotions. But they felt more positive emotions. This increase in positive emotions came from feeling good, not avoiding feeling bad.

Self- vs. Other-Validated Caregiving

When children are raised by violent, addicted, or chronically anxious caregivers, the experience attachment trauma—they are not able to reap the benefits of secure attachment that include regulated ANS functioning, sense of adequacy, ability to take healthy risks, and high relational functioning. Instead, they are watchful and scanning of their environment and the people in it. They are chronically anxious and on guard in the context of other people.

These children, early on, learn the skill of "exquisite attunement" to their caregivers. They intuitively know that when their caregiver is anxious, sad, angry, or in some other uncomfortable emotional state, it will soon mean a painful experience for them. So, as an instinctual adaptation to this dangerous environment, children are intuitively alerted when their caregivers are uncomfortable and begin to engage in a set of behaviors to soothe their parents. By the time they are launched into adolescence, these children are experts at reading others and very adept at quickly building emotional and support connections with others. They are expert counselors, nurses, and first responders before they ever take their first college or training course.

These young adults have a lifetime of helping already behind them, and many have used this altruistic helping as a tool for navigating the difficult social climate of junior high and high school. They simply supplied their friends with whatever they needed or wanted to assure they would not be betrayed, ridiculed or abandoned. And this skill served them well. Freud said the three healthy ego defenses were humor, art, and altruism.

As these young adults matriculated through their training programs to become counselors, physicians, nurses, etc., they found themselves in a role they had already been practicing for years. They already had many of the basic relational competencies that others had to study and practice.

Activity

Letter from the Great Supervisor

Imagine you could get a letter from the greatest supervisor of all time, whoever that is. In that letter, you find all of the validation you ever wanted to hear from an external source. Write a letter to yourself cleanly and clearly. Articulate to yourself from the voice of this great supervisor how precious, valuable, and important you are for making a difference in the world. You do not need to share this with anyone.

_____

_____

_____

_____

_____

_____

_____

_____

_____

_____

_____

_____

_____

_____

_____

_____

Notes:

Resilience Skill 4: Connection and Support

Education

Identity

Activity

Sharing

The importance of working within a community and being able to utilize that community for our own support is essential. Why is it that good therapists see a colleague on a regular basis? We simply cannot do good caregiving work in isolation. We need to intentionally utilize a care network made up of individuals we trust and respect. We need to turn to these individuals on a regular basis (weekly, biweekly, or monthly, depending upon the intensity of our caregiving work) to receive support and to dilute the effects of our work.

We have identified four important functions of a support network:

Sharing Trauma Narratives (applies to exposure to both primary and secondary trauma)

Telling our stories is healing, especially for symptoms of secondary traumatic stress disorder. We have found that people exposed to trauma have an intense need to make sense of what happened to them. Sharing traumatic experiences helps a person organize memories into a manageable and understandable "package." Research performed with medical doctors indicated that the single most effective preventative technique to avoid compassion fatigue was peer support through telling a narrative.

By sharing our narratives, we are able to relegate traumatic experiences to the past so that they stop intruding into the present and impeding our intention. We need to regularly share with our support group the parts of our personal or professional experience that are intruding into our thoughts and dreams. These may be personal traumas from our own past or present, or they may be experiences that we have witnessed either through our work on a trauma site or through the narratives of the people we help. Anything that is still causing us discomfort is appropriate for this exercise.

Empowering to Confront

It is nearly impossible to see the ways in which we are affected by the secondary traumatic stress and perceived threat associated with our work. Add to this the fact that most of us have learned to deny our symptoms until they begin to produce crisis, and you have a fertile breeding ground for compassion fatigue. That is why it is important to pick two or three folks from our support network and empower them to confront us when they see us (a) becoming symptomatic and/or (b) habitually breaching our integrity. You will want to empower them to push through your defenses, remind you of your covenant, and "get in your face" even if you get irritated with them.

Telling on Ourselves

Hopefully, through this program we have begun to see the futility of avoidance, denial, suppression, and procrastination as stress-management strategies. We do not have to look too deeply to see that these strategies actually increase our levels of perceived threat and lower our resilience. Secrecy is a potent virus that causes spiritual sickness. We want to be free of these ills, and for that reason we see the value in externalizing and sharing with our trusted network the places that we are engaging in habitual breaches of our integrity. As we begin to engage in this proactive self-care, it gives us a good, clean feeling that we are maturing as we turn away from our old ineffective coping and toward our own integrity.

Accountability

After we "tell on ourselves," our support network can become a source of accountability as they witness the commitment we make with ourselves to bring our behavior into alignment with our code of honor. They can gently remind us by periodically asking us how we are doing in this particular area. We are much more likely to follow through on commitments that have been witnessed by others.

Training Your Network

It is your responsibility to train your support network to be maximally supportive. If you have been careful in your selection of support persons, then you will have selected people who sincerely want to help. However, most others simply do not know how to be helpful to you and, in their anxiety to be helpful, can make things even worse. Chances are they perceive threat while wondering if they are really being helpful for you. You can help them to relax and be certain that you are getting the maximum from your meeting time if you will take a little time on the front end to let them know what you are doing and how they can be most helpful.

The following script has been offered as a suggestion for developing your support network:

Hey, I just learned that I might be high-risk for compassion fatigue. And that preventing compassion fatigue requires that I regularly share my narratives with another person. I'd like for you to be that person. If you are willing, I'd like to show you this thing I learned about how to keep your body relaxed while you are listening to me so that you don't get sick with my stories [teach pelvic floor relaxation]. I promise you I will always ask permission from you and allow you time to prepare yourself before I start talking with you about these issues—I won't hijack you. I would ask that you make yourself available sometime within seventy-two hours, either in person or by telephone. When we meet, I will have not interrupt. If you have insights, comments, or suggestions, I would love to hear them—after I have completed my narrative.

If you are willing to do this for me, then I will reciprocate. I will offer the same thing— I only ask that you ask me first and I will make myself available to you within seventy two hours.

Now, all that is left to do is schedule your first meeting …

Building Your Network

On the lines below, list three people whom you would like to include as part of your support network.

_____

_____

_____

_____

_____

Resilience Skill 5:
Self-Care and Revitalization

Education

Identity

Activity

Sharing

"What is to give light must endure burning."

This quote from Viktor Frankl has become the essence of our work with resilience. It contains two important concepts. First, the burning. In this, Dr. Frankl is telling those of us who have chosen to be givers of light that we are going to experience some burn. It is inevitable that we are going to experience pain from our work of fixing the broken, healing the sick, comforting the lost, and witnessing the dying. And to endure this burning, we must become more relaxed, more mature in our perceptions, and resilient enough that witnessing and absorbing pain does not diminish us.

The second part of this quote, however, has to do with refueling. If we are going to burn, then we need to be burning fuel, not ourselves. If we are burning only ourselves without stocking up on physical and emotional fuel, we won't burn very brightly or for very long. It is essential we develop a systematic discipline of refueling ourselves physically, emotionally, psychologically, spiritually, relationally, and professionally.

There are myriad ways in which we can achieve this refueling and revitalization. For some, the process is more physical in nature, while for others it is more intellectual, and still others use artistic expression or a combination of means. It is our responsibility to discover and then regularly practice what best works for us to sustain our energy, buoyancy, and hope.

What is self-care? Self-care is engaging in behaviors that balance the effects of emotional and physical stressors. This includes, but is not limited to a nutritious diet, preventative medicine, aerobic exercise, getting enough sleep, creativity, and relaxation. It means listening to our bodies, abstaining from substance abuse, and engaging in meaningful connections with others who support us. Changing our behaviors can be challenging and often requires commitment, discipline, and ongoing attention and care.

Self-care is more than bubble baths and dark chocolate. There is nothing wrong with bubble baths, chocolate, massages, and other luxuries. They can be lovely temporary mood boosters, but they don't offer the sustained long-term benefits of true self-care. Self-care is not self-indulgence. Too frequently these terms are used interchangeably. Self-indulgence is often about avoiding the effort of true self-care and settling for quick, largely symbolic "fixes" that may stress our system further.

Essential Components of Good Self-Care

While what works to keep someone energized and revitalized is very individual, some commonalities do exist. They are:

- Regular (three times weekly) aerobic activity

- Healthy diet

- Good sleep hygiene

- Regular social activities

- Creative activity or hobbies

- Spiritual practices

- Professional enrichment

These are only common examples. Do those that work best for you. It is your responsibility to find and implement a program of self-care and revitalization that you feel comfortable participating in.

Activity

Self-Care Assessment

Look at the items listed on the next two pages. Write down in the blank beside each item how frequently you engage in the activity. Then circle one from each heading that you can commit to improving over the next month.

1=Never   2=Rarely   3=Sometimes   4=Often   5=Very Often

Physical Self-Care

_____Aerobic activity 3x per week

_____Eat regularly, 3 meals per day

_____Eat healthy foods

_____Tone muscles

_____Use preventative medical care

_____Get medical care when needed

_____Take time off work when sick

_____Get massages to relax muscles

_____Dance, swim, walk, run, play sports, or do other

　　　　physical activities you enjoy

_____Take time to be sexual

_____Get enough sleep

_____Wear clothes you like

_____Take vacations

Spiritual Self-Care

_____Spend time in nature

_____Find a spiritual connection or community

_____Cherish optimism and hope

_____Be open to not knowing

_____Sing

_____Pray

_____Spend time with children

_____Be open to inspiration

_____Have gratitude

1=Never   2=Rarely   3=Sometimes   4=Often   5=Very Often

_____Meditate

_____Listen to music

_____Engage in an artistic activity

_____Yoga

_____Have experiences of awe

_____Be mindful of what is happening in your body and around you

_____Make meanings from difficulties

_____Seek truth

Emotional Self-Care

_____Connect with others whose company you enjoy

_____Love yourself

_____Laugh

_____Cry

_____Play with animals

_____Play with children

_____Express anger in social action (letters to newspapers, posts on social
          media, make donations)

_____Be of service to others

Psychological Self-Care

_____Relax your muscles at work

_____Relax your muscles in your personal life

_____Make time away from demands

_____Write in a journal

_____Read literature that is unrelated to work

_____Do something at which you are not an expert or in charge

_____Let others know different aspects of you

_____Be curious

_____Say no to extra responsibilities

_____Decrease stress in your life

1=Never   2=Rarely   3=Sometimes   4=Often   5=Very Often

Professional Self-Care

_____Take time to eat lunch

_____Take time to connect with coworkers

_____Make quiet time to complete tasks

_____Identify projects or tasks that are exciting/rewarding

_____Set limits with clients and colleagues

_____Balance your workload so that you are not overwhelmed

_____Arrange your workspace so that it is comfortable

_____Get regular consultation and supervision

_____Negotiate your needs (benefits, pay raises, etc.)

_____Go on a peer support group or outing

Other

Adapted from Saakvitne, K. W., Gamble, S., Pearlman, L. A., & Lev, B. T. (2000), *Risking Connection: A Training Curriculum for Working Survivors of Childhood Sexual Abuse***.**

Activity

Self-Directed Compassion Fatigue Resilience Plan

Having a compassion fatigue resilience plan in place puts your intentions into writing and improves the effectivenss of your efforts. Complete this plan for yourself using all of the information and techniques you have learned in this workbook.

1. **Self-regulation** is the ability to switch from the sympathetic to parasympathetic nervous system after you have determined that you are safe from threat. It requires relaxation of muscles. Identify method(s) that you will employ to relax your body and maintain its relaxation:

_____

_____

_____

_____

2. **Intentionality** is the ability to follow your Covenant/Code of Honor and maintain your personal integrity and to shift from reactivity and impulsive behaviors to chosen behaviors. Identify two situations where you perceive threat and you respond reactively, which derails you from accomplishing your mission and breaches your integrity. This example can be professional or personal. Make a commitment to self-regulate during these periods:

1. _____

2. _____

3. **Perceptual maturation** is evolving our perception to see our workplaces as less threatening and ourselves as empowered in these contexts. It is an important part of professional resiliency.

Identify one way that you can address each of the below in your work:

a. Choice vs. Demand:

b. Process vs. Outcomes:

c. Relinquishing Entitlement:

d. Maintaining Integrity:

e. Self-Validation:

f. Positive Outlook:

4. **Connection/support through narrative sharing** requires the utilization of three or more peers to serve as a support for you. These persons should be educated in how to best help you and should be able to listen without judgment or interruption. You will want these peers to be "safe" for you and trusted enough that you can share uncomfortable information. You will want to utilize these peers to discuss the painful and difficult aspects of your work and for discussions of where you are finding yourself struggling with intentionality. Identify three new people who you will request to become members of your support family:

1. _____

2. _____

3. _____

5. **Self-care.** What activities "refuel" you? You should identify at least one aerobic activity in which you will engage three times weekly. You should also identify an "integrative activity" (e.g., learning a musical instrument, learning an art or craft, learning a sport) that contains both the learning and discipline of mastering the rudiments (e.g., scales, tools, drills) as well as ample time to participate in "playing" in this activity. The remaining activities should replenish you and give you a sense of joy, reconnecting you with life, hope, and wonder. In total, you will have seven activities that will help you face each new day with fullness and potency:

a. Aerobic: _____

b. Physical: _____

c. Psychological: _____

d. Emotional: _____

e. Spiritual: _____

f. Professional: _____

g. Integrative: _____

Conclusion

Before we conclude our time together, we would like to take a moment to honor you and all you have given of yourself. Many of you reading this have been serving others for years, some for decades. Most of you have also discovered this service came with a cost. Some of you have lost things precious to you because of your continued commitment to this mission—like relationships, marriages, and health. Many of you have suffered physical, emotional, mental, and spiritual maladies as you have continued along your path of making lives a little better for others. No matter who you are or how long you have been engaged in professional or volunteer caregiving, this work has come with a personal cost to you. And yet you have persevered.

Even when it was inconvenient for you, even when it hurt, you continued being of service to others. You have shown up in the lives of people for whom no one else shows up. You have answered the late-night telephone calls; you have shown up at the emergency rooms; you have set aside your issues and priorities to bring some comfort and light to those who would not be receiving it from anyone else. Because you have remained true to your mission—even when it caused you pain—we would like for you to know that it has made a difference.

There are people out here in the world who, had you not shown up for them in the ways that you have, would be dead today. You physically saved their lives. Maybe you are a physician or nurse who successfully treated a life-threatening illness. Or maybe you are a mental health professional who intervened with a client who was contemplating suicide. Or maybe you were simply a friend who helped another friend find enough hope and stamina to walk through a daunting life crisis. Chances are there is at least one person out here somewhere who is still alive because you cared.

There are scores of others out here who—because you used every resource available to you, your charm, your persuasive capacities, your technical skills, and your love— are not in prison today. They are not self-destructively using chemicals. They are not prostituting their bodies or their principles. Because you showed up in their lives, they are, right now, in pursuit of their dreams. You brought this gift to them.

There are thousands of people out here who, because you intervened in their lives or the lives of their loved ones, are enjoying a better quality of life today. And it is your fault. You are changing the world. You are evolving our species. You are making a difference. And while it is sometimes difficult to see, you have been a faithful servant to others and remained true to your mission.

Which brings us to the most important thing we have to tell you, the most important information for you to take from this course—and that is THANK YOU. Thank you for making our world a little bit better place to live. Thank you for changing the world. Well done, good and faithful servant! As you read this, we invite you to reflect back on the faces of all those to whom you have provided service and hear from them the echoes of gratitude for your caring in their lives.

We hope that you are now prepared to go forth into this new chapter of your caregiving service, equipped with skills that allow you to continue this service without suffering, without generating symptoms. We hope that you are able to find that you can fully commit to your mission with a grateful heart and that you, like Viktor Frankl, are finding joy, peace, purpose, meaning, and love along your journey.

If you are interested in continuing this journey of resilience and optimization, we invite you to become a Certified Compassion Fatigue Specialist through the Trauma Institute International and Arizona Trauma Institute. This distance-learning course deepens your knowledge and understanding of compassion fatigue and prepares you to bring information and relief to others suffering the effects of work-related stress. You can find more information at www.aztrauma.org and www.traumainstituteinternational.com.

Finally, we would like to remind you that we are here for you. We are working to build an intentional and sustainable community of trauma professionals at AZ Trauma. We would love to have you involved. Should you find yourself suffering from your work—professional or volunteer—of being of service to others, please contact us. We promise that we will help you find the resources to help you continue your mission without suffering. You may use the contact information below.

J. Eric Gentry, PhD
Vice President
Arizona Trauma Institute / Trauma Institute International
PO Box 937
Phoenix, AZ 85001
www.aztrauma.org
www.traumainstituteinternational.com
j.eric.gentry.phd@gmail.com
eric.gentry@aztrauma.org

Marette Monson, LCSW
Center for Counseling Excellence
www.centerforcounselingexcellence.com
www.marettemonson.com
Marette.Monson@gmail.com

Healing Trauma With Intentional Living Worksheet

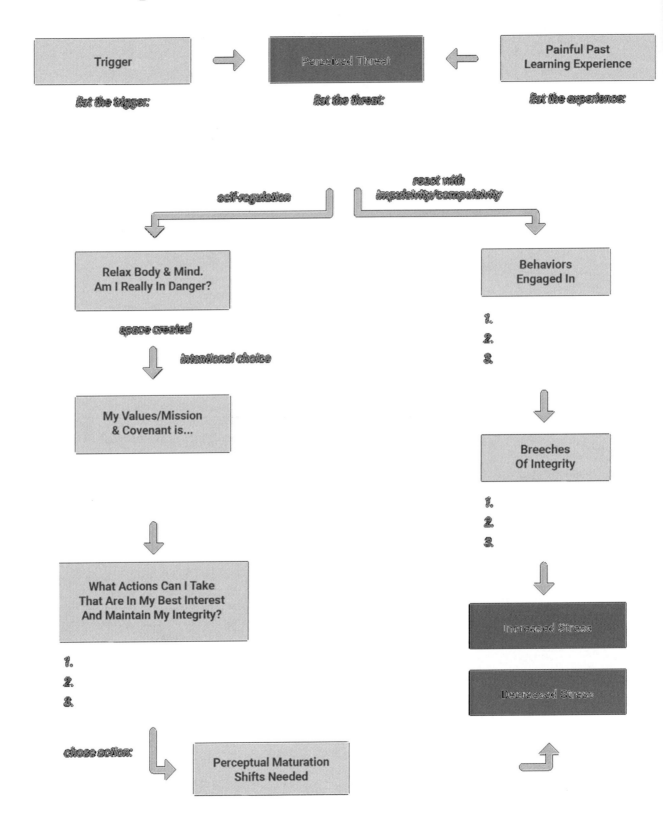

Trigger → Perceived Threat ← Painful Past Learning Experience

list the trigger: *list the threat:*   *list the experience:*

self-regulation   *react with impulsivity/compulsivity*

Relax Body & Mind. Am I Really In Danger?

space created   *intentional choice*

My Values/Mission & Covenant is...

What Actions Can I Take That Are In My Best Interest And Maintain My Integrity?

1.
2.
3.

chose action:

Perceptual Maturation Shifts Needed

Behaviors Engaged In

1.
2.
3.

Breeches Of Integrity

1.
2.
3.

Increased Stress

Decreased Stress

Putting It All Together

Use the worksheet to apply the concepts you learned in this workbook to your work stress. An example of a completed worksheet is on the next page.

Follow the steps below:

1. Under the box labeled "Trigger," list a few things that happen in your professional life that cause you stress.

2. Think about the painful past learning experience you had where those things happened. Find the box on the right side of the paper labeled "Painful Past Learning Experience" and write a few words describing the experience underneath the box. Your painful past learning joins with a trigger to activate a perceived threat.

3. Write the perceived threat to your ego or your physical well-being under the box labeled "Perceived Threat." At this point, you have a decision to make. You can either choose to self-regulate or you can choose to react with impulsivity and compulsivity. When you react in an impulsive or compulsive way, what behaviors do you engage in? List those.

4. When you engage in those behaviors, what breaches of integrity are present? List those. Breaches of integrity lead to increased stress at work and at home. They create compassion fatigue. Now go back and instead choose to regulate your body by relaxing and reminding yourself you are not in real danger. This action creates a space in which we can have some time to make an intentional choice, rather than react impulsively.

5. List the intentional choice you would like to make in the situation.

6. List the values/mission or covenant you have that guides the interactions you have professionally.

7. List some actions you can choose to take that would allow you to remain true to that mission/covenant. Those actions will shift your perception of the event so that it is no longer viewed as a threat. Because you acted according to your integrity and shifted your perception, your stress level at work will be decreased.

Share this worksheet with your compassion fatigue buddy and discuss each of the areas. As a new stressor pops up at work, feel free to complete another worksheet to keep the dialogue with your compassion fatigue buddy open and your commitment to intentionally choose another choice fresh in your mind. As you apply these concepts, you will be able to do what you love to do professionally and remain stress free!

Healing Trauma With Intentional Living Worksheet

Trigger → **Perceived Threat** ← **Painful Past Learning Experience**

list the trigger:

Missing a deadline because a client was in crisis and I dropped everything to respond to it.

list the threat:

I'm going to fail / I am a failure. I am responsible for my client's choices.

list the experience:

Almost didn't graduate high school because I didn't get work turned in on time because I was caring for a parent with cancer.

self-regulation

react with impulsivity/compulsivity

Relax Body & Mind. Am I Really In Danger?

Behaviors Engaged In

1. Procrastination / avoiding the task
2. Find other things to fill my time
3. Yell at spouse / kids for not doing responsibilities at home

space created

intentional choice

My Values/Mission & Covenant is...

To respond, resource and react with kindness and consistency to clients, co-workers and family.

Breeches Of Integrity

1. Not treating others with respect
2. Not doing what I say I'm going to do
3. Lying to boss about why it isn't done

What Actions Can I Take That Are In My Best Interest And Maintain My Integrity?

1. Take accountability. Call my boss and admit I missed the deadline.
2. Eliminate distractions so I can get it done.
3. Ask for help from others to manage my priorities and clients

Increased Stress

Decreased Stress

chose action:

All three!

Perceptual Maturation Shifts Needed

I am responsible for the quality of my work, but not the outcome.

Appendix

J. Eric Gentry, PhD, LMHC, CAC

Compassion Unlimited

PO Box 937
Phoenix, AZ 85001

eg@compassionunlimited.com
www.compassionunlimited.com

Acknowledgements: The author wishes to acknowledge support for this article from Anna Baranowsky, PhD, private practice, Toronto, Canada.

Abstract

This article explores the history, causes, treatments and prevention of compassion fatigue, the negative effects of helping others, contexualized for application to the trauma recovery efforts from the events of September 11, 2001. The author draws upon experience with development and implementation of the Accelerated Recovery Program for Compassion Fatigue, the Certified Compassion Fatigue Specialist Training, and the provision of treatment and training to hundreds of caregivers suffering from compassion fatigue symptoms. A model for understanding the multiple causes of compassion fatigue is presented, along with distillation of the active ingredients for effective treatment and prevention of its symptoms. Symptoms of compassion fatigue are conceptualized not only as disruptive and deleterious effects of caring for the traumatized, but also as a catalyst for positive change, transformation, maturation, and resiliency in the lives of these caregivers. Specific suggestions for compassion fatigue prevention and resiliency are reviewed.

Introduction

On October 19, 2001, I co-facilitated a Critical Incident Stress Debriefing (CISD; Mitchell, 1995) in New York City for 12 mid-level retail managers who had been working two blocks from the World Trade Center on September 11, 2001. As this group navigated through the CISD and its cognitive-affective-cognitive "schwoop" (Norman, 2001), that hallmark of emergency psychology, one person began to describe the debris falling from the crumbling towers by saying, "in my mind I see chunks of concrete falling from the building but I know it was really people that I saw falling … jumping." As she spoke, I could not help myself from forming my own images of falling debris coalescing into anatomical features. Another participant reported that the worst part of September Eleventh for him was the emergence of recurrent intrusive images and nightmares. However, the intrusions he was experiencing were not of the horrors he saw in lower Manhattan; instead they were of tracer rounds from automatic rifles firing over his and his mother's head when he was a child fleeing Vietnam in 1975. As he described the spontaneous emergence of these memories, brought to consciousness for the first time in 26 years, I began to recall images from some of the thousands of combat trauma narratives I have heard from the hundreds of combat veterans that I have treated. I also began to feel some anxiety for the co-facilitator who was leading this debriefing, as this was his thirtieth straight day of providing trauma relief services in New York City and he was a Vietnam combat veteran.

While participating in this debriefing, I was acutely aware of my powerlessness to prevent the images, thoughts and feelings shared by the participants from finding their way into parallel associations in my own consciousness. Having spent the past five years studying and treating compassion fatigue, I knew that I was high risk for the development of secondary traumatic stress symptoms. For the next several weeks I experienced recurrent images and accompanying arousal from this and other experiences in New York. It was only after extensive support from colleagues and my work, as a client, with Eye Movement Desensitization & Reprocessing (EMDR, Shapiro, 1995), that I was able to relegate these images and feelings from the encroaching present into the near-distant past.

Thousands of emergency service and mental health professionals have labored heroically to assist survivors of the events of 9/11/01. These service professionals have witnessed events and heard stories of incredible courage and resiliency in the course of providing assistance to the survivors. They have also been exposed to incidents and reports of life-shattering pain, terror, and loss. There is no doubt that there are great rewards associated with providing care and assistance to survivors of trauma; for those of us who have chosen traumatology as a professional path, there is no sweeter experience than witnessing a survivor emerge transformed and fortified from the dark jungle of posttraumatic symptoms. There is also, however, little doubt that serving these survivors exacts a toll that while minimal for some caregivers, can be devastating for others. As Viktor Frankl, one of the twentieth century's greatest traumatologists, simultaneously warns and encourages: *"**That which is to give light must endure burning**"* (Frankl, 1963, p. 129).

This article explores the potential causes, prevention, and treatments of compassion fatigue (Figley, 1995), the deleterious effects of helping the traumatized, as it relates to the tragedy of September 11, 2001. It is offered with the hope that it may help some of those dedicated to being of service to survivors in New York and across the nation to continue being givers of light, burning ever more brightly, and never burning out.

Compassion Fatigue

The notion that working with people in pain extracts a significant cost from the caregiver is not new. Although the costs vary and have been lamented from time immemorial, anyone who has sat at the bedside of a seriously ill or recently bereaved loved one knows the toll involved in devoting singular attention to the needs of another suffering person. Only in recent years, however, has there been a substantial effort to examine the effects on the caregiver of bearing witness to the indescribable wounds inflicted by traumatic experiences. The exploration and examination of these effects evolved throughout the last century and comes to us from a wide variety of sources.

One of the first earliest references in the scientific literature regarding this cost of caring comes from Carl G. Jung in **The Psychology of Dementia Praecox** (Jung, 1907). In this text, Jung discusses the challenges of **countertransference** — the therapist's conscious and unconscious reactions to the patient in the therapeutic situation — and the particular countertransferential difficulties analysts encounter when working with psychotic patients. He boldly **prescribes** a treatment stance in which the therapist participates in the delusional fantasies and hallucinations with the patient. Nevertheless, he warns that this participation in the patient's darkly painful fantasy world of traumatic images has significant deleterious effects for the therapist, especially the neophyte and/or the therapist who has not resolved his/her own developmental and traumatic issues (Sedgewick, 1995).

The study of countertransference produced the first writings in the field of psychotherapy that systematically explored the effects of psychotherapy upon the therapist (Haley, 1974; Danieli, 1982; Lindy, 1988; Wilson & Lindy, 1994; Karakashian, 1994; Pearlman & Saakvitne, 1995). Recent texts have suggested that therapists sometimes experience countertransference reactions that imitate the symptoms of their clients (Herman, 1992; Pearlman & Saakvitne, 1995). For instance, when working with survivors of traumatic experiences, authors have reported countertransference phenomena that mimic the symptoms of posttraumatic stress disorder (PTSD; Lindy, 1988; Wilson & Lindy, 1994; Pearlman & Saakvitne, 1995).

Business and industry, with their progressive focus upon productivity in the last half of the twentieth century, have provided us with the concept of burnout (Fruedenberger, 1974; Maslach, 1976) to describe the deleterious effects the environmental demands of the workplace have on the worker. Burnout, or "the syndrome of emotional exhaustion, depersonalization, and reduced personal accomplishment" (Maslach, 1976, p. 56), has been used to describe the chronic effects that psychotherapists suffer as a result of interactions with their clients and/or the demands of their workplace (Freudenberger, 1974; Cherniss, 1980; Farber, 1983; Sussman, 1992; Grosch & Olsen, 1995; Maslach & Goldberg, 1998). Research has shown that therapists are particularly vulnerable to burnout because of personal isolation, ambiguous successes and the emotional drain of remaining empathetic (McCann & Pearlman, 1990). Moreover, burnout not only is psychologically debilitating to therapists, but also impairs the therapist's capacity to deliver competent mental health services (Farber, 1983). The literature on burnout, with its twenty-five year history, thoroughly describes the phenomena and prescribes preventive and treatment interventions for helping professionals.

The study of the effects of trauma has also promoted a better understanding of the negative effects of helping. Psychological reactions to trauma have been described over the past one hundred and fifty years by various names such as "shell shock", "combat neurosis", "railroad spine", and "combat fatigue" (Shalev, Bonne, & Eth, 1996). However, not until 1980 was the latest designation for these reactions, posttraumatic stress disorder (PTSD), formally recognized as an anxiety disorder in the Diagnostic and Statistical Manual of Mental Disorders-III (DSM-III, American Psychiatric Association, 1980; Matsakis, 1994). Since that time, research into posttraumatic stress has grown at an exponential rate (Figley, 1995; Wilson & Lindy, 1994) and the field of traumatology has been established with two of it's own journals, several professional organizations, and unique professional identity (Figley, 1988; Bloom, 1999; Gold & Faust, 2001).

As therapists are increasingly called upon to assist survivors of violent crime, natural disasters, childhood abuse, torture, acts of genocide, political persecution, war, and now terrorism (Sexton, 1999), discussion regarding the reactions of therapists and other helpers to working with trauma survivors has recently emerged in the traumatology literature (Figley, 1983, 1995; Danieli, 1988; McCann & Pearlman, 1990; Pearlman & Saakvitne, 1995; Stamm, 1995). Professionals who listen to reports of trauma, horror, human cruelty and extreme loss can become overwhelmed and may begin to experience feelings of fear, pain and suffering similar to that of their clients. They may also experience PTSD symptoms similar to their clients', such as intrusive thoughts, nightmares, avoidance and arousal, as well as changes in their relationships to their selves, their families, friends and communities (Figley, 1995; McCann & Pearlman, 1990, Salston, 1999).Therefore, they may themselves come to need assistance to cope with the effects of listening to others' traumatic experiences (Figley, 1995; Pearlman & Saakvitne, 1995; Saakvitne, 1996; Gentry, Baranowsky & Dunning,1997, in press).

While the empirical literature has been slow to develop in this area, there is an emerging body of scientific publications that attempts to identify and define the traumatization of helpers through their efforts of helping. Pearlman and Saakvitne (1995), Figley (1995), and Stamm (1995) all authored and/or edited texts that explored this phenomenon among helping professionals during the same pivotal year. The terms "vicarious traumatization" (McCann & Pearlman, 1990; Pearlman & Saakvitne, 1995), "secondary traumatic stress" (Figley, 1987; Stamm, 1995) and "compassion fatigue" (Figley, 1995) have all become cornerstones in the vernacular of describing the deleterious effects that helpers suffer when working with trauma survivors.

Vicarious traumatization (McCann & Pearlman, 1990) refers to the transmission of traumatic stress through observation and/or hearing others' stories of traumatic events and the resultant shift/distortions that occur in the caregiver's perceptual and meaning systems. Secondary traumatic stress occurs when one is exposed to extreme events directly experienced by another and becomes overwhelmed by this secondary exposure to trauma (Figley & Kleber, 1995). Several theories have been offered but none has been able to conclusively demonstrate the mechanism that accounts for the transmission of traumatic stress from one individual to another. It has been hypothesized that the caregiver's level of empathy with the traumatized individual plays a significant role in this transmission (Figley ,1995) and some budding empirical data to support this hypothesis (Salston, 2000).

Figley (1995) also proposes that the combined effects of the caregiver's continuous visualizing of clients' traumatic images added to the effects of burnout can create a condition progressively debilitating the caregiver that he has called "compassion stress." This construct holds that exposure to clients' stories of traumatization can produce a form of posttraumatic stress disorder in which Criterion A, or "the event" criterion, is met through listening to, instead of the in vivo experiencing of, a traumatic event. The symptoms of compassion fatigue, divided into categories of intrusive, avoidance, and arousal symptoms, are summarized in Table I.

Table I: Compassion Fatigue Symptoms

Intrusive Symptoms
• Thoughts and images associated with client's traumatic experiences
• Obsessive and compulsive desire to help certain clients
• Client/work issues encroaching upon personal time
• Inability to "let go" of work-related matters
• Perception of survivors as fragile and needing the assistance of caregiver ("savior")
• Thoughts and feelings of inadequacy as a caregiver
• Sense of entitlement or special-ness
• Perception of the world in terms of victims and perpetrators
• Personal activities interrupted by work-related issues

Avoidance Symptoms
• Silencing Response (avoiding hearing/witnessing client's traumatic material)
• Loss of enjoyment in activities/cessation of self care activities
• Loss of energy
• Loss of hope/sense of dread working with certain clients
• Loss of sense of competence/potency
• Isolation
• Secretive self-medication/addiction (alcohol, drugs, work, sex, food, spending, etc)
• Relational dysfunction

Arousal Symptoms
• Increased anxiety
• Impulsivity/reactivity
• Increased perception of demand/threat (in both job and environment)
• Increased frustration/anger
• Sleep disturbance
• Difficulty concentrating
• Change in weight/appetite
• Somatic symptoms

As a result of our work with hundreds of caregivers suffering the effects of compassion fatigue, we have augmented Figley's (1995) definition to include pre-existing and/or concomitant primary posttraumatic stress and its symptoms. Many caregivers, especially those providing on-site services, will have had first-hand exposure to the traumatic event(s) to which they are responding (Pole et al., 2001; Marmar et al., 1999). For many, these symptoms of PTSD will have a delayed onset and not become manifest until some time later. We have also found that many caregivers enter the service field with a host of traumatic experiences in their developmental past (Gentry, 1999). There may have been no symptoms associated with these events, or the symptoms related to them may have remained sub-clinical. However, we have observed that as these caregivers begin to encounter the traumatic material presented by clients, many of them begin to develop clinical PTSD symptoms associated with their previously "benign" historical experiences. In our efforts to treatment compassion fatigue, we have concluded that it is often necessary to successfully address and resolve primary traumatic stress before addressing any issues of secondary traumatic stress and/or burnout. Additionally, we have discerned an interactive, or synergistic, effect among primary traumatic stress, secondary traumatic stress, and burnout symptoms in the life of an afflicted caregiver. Experiencing symptoms from any one of these three sources appears to diminish resiliency and lower thresholds for the adverse impact of the other two. This seems to lead to a rapid onset of severe symptoms that can become extremely debilitating to the caregiver within a very short period of time.

Table II: Compassion Fatigue Model

The Gentry/Baranowsky (1997) Model of Compassion Fatigue

PRIMARY TRAUMATIC STRESS

+/x (synergistic effect)

SECONDARY TRAUMATIC STRESS

+/x (synergistic effect)

BURNOUT

———————————————

COMPASSION FATIGUE

Accelerated Recovery Program for Compassion Fatigue

In 1997, two Green Cross Scholars and one doctoral student under the direction and supervision of Charles Figley at Florida State University developed the Accelerated Recovery Program for Compassion Fatigue (Gentry, Baranowsky & Dunning, 1997, in press; Gentry & Baranowsky, 1998, 1999, 1999a, 1999b). This five-session manualized and copyrighted protocol[2] was designed to address the symptoms of secondary traumatic stress and burnout, or compassion fatigue, in caregivers. Phase one clinical trials with this protocol was completed with the developers and seven volunteers from various disciplines and backgrounds who had experience working with trauma survivors.[3] The qualitative data obtained from these initial volunteers were utilized to create the final version of the protocol. Each of these participants reported clinically significant lessening of compassion fatigue symptoms with one exception.[4]

The Accelerated Recovery Program (ARP) was presented in the fall of 1997 at the International Society for Traumatic Stress Studies (ISTSS) in Montreal, Canada. In attendance at this presentation was an official with the Federal Bureau of Investigation who requested that the developers provide training to his staff, and, subsequent to this training, the Accelerated Recovery Program was adopted for use in this agency (McNally, 1998, personal communication). As a result of contacts made through the FBI, twelve professional helpers who have provided on-going assistance to the survivors of the bombing of the Murrah Building in Oklahoma City requested treatment for their compassion fatigue symptoms through the Traumatology Institute at Florida State University. The ARP provided statistically and clinically significant successful treatment for each of these professionals (Gentry, 2000). Subsequent presentations on the ARP at ISTSS meetings in 1998, 1999, and the development of the Certified Compassion Fatigue Specialist Training (CCFST) have lead to the successful treatment of hundreds of caregivers with compassion fatigue symptoms through the Accelerated Recovery Program all over the world.

Certified Compassion Fatigue Specialist Training: Training-as-Treatment

In late 1998, Gentry and Baranowsky, two of the developers of the Accelerated Recovery Program, were approached by the Traumatology Institute at Florida State University to create a training program for helping professionals interested in developing expertise in treating compassion fatigue. Through initial consultations, it was decided that the training would be designed around the ARP Model and that the participants would receive training on the implementation of the five sessions of this protocol. In addition, the training was designed to provide the participants with an in-depth understanding of the etiology, phenomenology and treatment/prevention of compassion fatigue, including secondary traumatic stress and burnout. The participants of this training would be certified by Florida State University's Traumatology Institute as Compassion Fatigue Specialists and authorized to implement the Accelerated Recovery Program for other caregivers suffering from compassion fatigue symptoms.

In their design of the program, the developers decided that the participants should receive first-hand experiential training for each of the interventions used in the Accelerated Recovery Program. With this in mind, the 17-hour training was developed and manualized (Gentry & Baranowsky, 1998; 1999a) with a focus upon the experiential components of the ARP. This phase in development of the Certified Compassion Fatigue Specialist Training (CCFST) was the first conceptualization of the *"training-as-treatment"* (Gentry, 2000) model for addressing the participants' symptoms of compassion fatigue. The rationale was that since the interventions of the ARP were effective working with individuals, the interventions would also be effective with these symptoms, albeit to a lesser degree, with the participants of the training.

It was then decided that the collection of baseline and outcome data would be conducted from the first training that was implemented in January of 1999. Baseline and post-training scores from compassion fatigue, compassion satisfaction and burnout subscales of the Compassion Satisfaction/Fatigue Self-Test (Figley, 1995; Figley & Stamm, 1996) were collected. Data were analyzed for 166 participants who successfully completed the CCFS Training between January 1999 and January 2001 (Gentry, 2000). The protocol demonstrated clinically and statically significant results ($p < .001$) when pre-training and post-training scores on the compassion fatigue, compassion satisfaction and burnout subscales of the Compassion Satisfaction/Fatigue Self-Test (Figley & Stamm, 1996) were compared.

---

[2] *Treatment Manual for Accelerated Recovery from Compassion Fatigue* (Gentry & Baranowsky, 1998) is available from Psych InK Resources, 45 Sheppard Ave., Suite 202, Toronto, Ontario, Canada, M2N 5W9.

[3] These trials were completed with volunteers who were Marriage & Family Therapists, a trauma therapist from South Africa, and a volunteer who had been providing relief work in Sarajevo.

[4] This participant uncovered a primary traumatic experience for which she was previously amnestic. She left the country before her primary or secondary trauma could be successfully addressed and resolved.

Treatment & Prevention: Active Ingredients

It has been demonstrated that the potential to develop negative symptoms associated with our work in providing services to trauma survivors, especially the symptoms of secondary traumatic stress, increases as our exposure to their traumatic material increases (McCann & Pearlman, 1990; Salston, 2000),. We believe that no one who chooses to work with trauma survivors is immune to the potential deleterious effects of this work. However, in our work with providing effective treatment to hundreds of caregivers with compassion fatigue symptoms, either individually through the ARP or in CCFS training groups, we have identified some enduring principles, techniques, and ingredients that seem to consistently lead to these positive treatment outcomes and enhanced resiliency.

Intentionality. Initiation of effective resolution of compassion fatigue symptoms requires specific recognition and acceptance of the symptoms and their causes by the caregiver, along with a decision to address and resolve these symptoms. Many caregivers who experience symptoms of compassion fatigue will attempt to ignore their distress until a threshold of discomfort is reached. For many caregivers this may mean that they are unable to perform their jobs as well as they once did or as well as they would like due to the symptoms they are experiencing. For others, it may entail the progressive debilitation associated with somatic symptoms or the embarrassment and pain associated with secretive self-destructive comfort-seeking behaviors. Whatever the impetus, we have found that successful amelioration of compassion fatigue symptoms requires that the caregiver intentionally acknowledge and address, rather than avoid, these symptoms and their causes. Additionally, we have found the use of goal-setting and the development of a personal/professional mission statement to be invaluable in moving away from the reactivity associated with the victimization of compassion fatigue and toward the resiliency and intentionality of mature caregiving.

Connection. One of the ways trauma seems to affect us all, caregivers included, is to leave us with a sense of disconnected isolation. A common thread we have found with sufferers of compassion fatigue symptoms has been the progressive loss in their sense of connection and community. Many caregivers become increasingly isolatory as their symptoms intensify. Fear of being perceived as weak, impaired, or incompetent by peers and clients, along with time constraints and loss of interest, have all been cited by caregivers suffering from compassion fatigue as reasons for diminished intimate and collegial connection.

The development and maintenance of healthy relationships, which the caregiver uses for both support and to share/dilute the images and stories associated with secondary traumatic stress, may become a powerful mitigating factor in resolving and preventing compassion fatigue symptoms. Often the bridge for this connection is established in the peer-to-peer offering of the ARP, during which the facilitator works intentionally to develop a strong relationship with the caregiver suffering compassion fatigue symptoms. In the CCFST, we facilitate exercises specifically designed to dismantle interpersonal barriers and enhance self-disclosure. It seems that it is through these relational connections that the caregivers suffering compassion fatigue are able to gain insight and understanding that their symptoms are not an indication of some pathological weakness or disease, but are instead natural consequences of providing care for traumatized individuals. In addition, with the enhanced self-acceptance attained through self-disclosure with and by empathetic and understanding peers, caregivers are able to begin to see their symptoms as indicators of the developmental changes needed in both their self-care and caregiving practices. We have seen that a warm, supportive environment in which caregivers are able to discuss intrusive traumatic material, difficult clients, symptoms, fears, shame, and secrets with peers to be one of the most critical ingredients in the resolution and continued prevention of compassion fatigue.

Anxiety Management/Self-Soothing. It is our belief that providing caregiving services while experiencing intense anxiety is one of the primary means by which compassion fatigue symptoms are contracted and exacerbated. Alternately stated, to the degree that a caregiver is able to remain non-anxious (relaxed pelvic floor muscles), we believe, s/he will maintain resistance to the development of symptoms of compassion fatigue. The ability to self-regulate and soothe anxiety and stress is thought to be a hallmark of maturity. The mastery of these skills comes only with years of practice. However, if we fail to develop the capacity for self-regulation, if we are unable to internally attenuate our own levels of arousal, then we are susceptible to perceiving as threats those people, objects, and situations to which we respond with anxiety — believing that benign people, objects and situations are dangerous. As one very insightful and astute psychologist who was a participant in the CCFST stated: "Maybe the symptoms of compassion fatigue are a good thing, they force us to become stronger." It does seem to be true that those caregivers with well-developed self-regulation skills who do not resort to self-destructive and addictive comfort-seeking behaviors are unlikely to suffer symptoms of compassion fatigue.

In both the ARP and the CCFST, we work rigorously with participant caregivers to help them develop self-management plans that will assist them in achieving and maintaining an *in vivo* non-anxious presence. This non-anxious presence extends far beyond a calm outward appearance. Instead, it entails the ability to maintain a level of relaxed mindfulness and comfort in one's own body. This ability to remain non-anxious when confronted with the pain, horror, loss, and powerlessness associated with the traumatic experiences in the lives of clients of having the capacity to calmly "bear witness," remains a key ingredient in the resolution and prevention of compassion fatigue symptoms.

Self-Care. Closely associated with self-management is the concept of self-care or the ability to refill and refuel oneself in healthy ways. It is quite common for caregivers to find themselves anxious during and after working with severely traumatized individuals. Instead of developing a system of healthy practices for resolving this anxiety — such as sharing with colleagues, exercise, meditation, nutrition, and spirituality — many caregivers find themselves redoubling their work efforts. Frequently this constricting cycle of working harder in an attempt to feel better creates a distorted sense of entitlement that can lead to a breach of personal and professional boundaries. We have worked with many caregivers who have reported falling prey to compulsive behaviors such as overeating, overspending, or alcohol/drug abuse in an effort to soothe the anxiety they feel from the perceived demands of their work. Others with whom we have worked have self-consciously admitted to breaching professional boundaries and ethics when at the low point in this cycle, distortedly believing that they "deserve" this "special" treatment or reward.

Meta-analyses of psychotherapy outcomes consistently point toward the quality of the relationship between therapist and client as the single most important ingredient in positive outcomes (Bergin & Garfield, 1994). The integrity and quality of this relationship is contingent upon the therapist's maintenance of his/her instrument, the "self of the therapist." When caregivers fail to maintain a life that is rich with meaning and gratification outside the professional arena, then they often look to work as the sole source of these commodities. In this scenario, caregivers interact with their clients from a stance of depletion and need. It is completely understandable that this orientation would produce symptoms in caregivers. Conversely, professionals who responsibly pursue and acquire this sense of aliveness outside the closed system of their professional role are able to engage in work with traumatized individuals while sharing their own fullness, meaning, and joy. The cycle of depletion by our work and intentionally refilling ourselves in our lives outside of work, often on a daily basis, may have been what Frankl meant when he challenged us to "endure burning."

One of the most important aspects of this category of self-care that we have found in our work with caregivers has been the development and maintenance of a regular exercise regimen. No other single behavior seems to be as important than regular aerobic and anaerobic activity. In addition to exercise, good nutrition, artistic expression/discipline (e.g., piano lessons and composition, dance classes and choreography, structural planning and building), meditation/mindfulness, outdoor recreation, and spirituality all seem to be important ingredients to a good self-care plan.

We have found a few caregivers with compassion fatigue symptoms that seemed to be at least partially caused by working beyond their level of skill. Working with traumatized individuals, families, and communities is a highly skilled activity that demands many years of training in many different areas before one gains a sense of mastery. Trying to shortcut this process by prematurely working with trauma survivors without adequate training and supervision can very easily overwhelm even seasoned clinicians, much less neophytes. While empirical research has not yet addressed the effects of working beyond levels of competency or of providing services while impaired with stress symptoms has upon the care provider, especially in contexts of mass casualties like we have witnessed in New York City, we believe that these factors contribute significantly to the frequency, duration and intensity of compassion fatigue symptoms.

Sometimes training in the area of treating trauma, especially experiential trainings such as EMDR (Shapiro, 1995) or TIR (French & Harris, 1998), can have a powerful ameliorative effect upon compassion fatigue, bringing a sense of empowerment to a caregiver who was previously overwhelmed. The caveat here is that there exists some danger that an overwhelmed therapist who has been recently trained in one of these powerful techniques may emerge from the training with an inflated sense skill and potency. Newly empowered, this therapist may be tempted to practice even further beyond their level of competence and skill. This scenario highlights the importance of good professional supervision during the developmental phases of a traumatologist's career. In addition, many therapists working with trauma survivors have found it helpful to receive periodic "check ups" with a trusted professional or peer supervisor. This is especially true during an immediately following deployment in a disaster or critical incident situation. hese professional and peer supervisory relationships can serve as excellent opportunities to share, and therefore dilute the effects, of the artifacts of secondary traumatic stress that may have been collected while in service to trauma survivors. Professional supervision is also reported to have an overall ameliorative effect upon compassion fatigue symptoms (Pearlman, 1995; Catherall, 1995).

Every caregiver's self-care needs are different. Some will need to remain vigilant in the monitoring and execution of their self-care plan, while others will, seemingly, be able to maintain resiliency with minimal effort. However, we strongly urge the caregiver who specializes working with trauma and trauma survivors to develop a comprehensive self-care plan that addresses and meets the caregiver's individual needs for each of the areas discussed in this article. With this self-care plan in place, the caregiver can now practice with the assurance that they are maximizing resiliency toward and prevention of the symptoms of compassion fatigue that is akin to the protection of wearing a seatbelt while driving an automobile.

It should be noted that those care providers responding on-site to crisis situations, such as those caused by the events of September 11, may be limited in their ability to employ habitual self-care activities. They may not have access to gymnasiums or exercise facilities, nutritious food and water may be scarce for a period of time, and it is doubtful that care providers deployed in situations of mass destruction will have access to their traditional support network. While most trauma responders are a hardy and resilient breed, we simply cannot sustain the rigors of this depleting and intensive work without intentional concern for our own health and welfare. Making best use of available resources to establish respite and sanctuary for ourselves, even in the most abject of circumstances, can have an enormous effect in minimizing our symptoms and maximizing our sustained effectiveness. Many responders have reported acts of kindness as simple as the gift of a bottle of water, a pat on the back, or an opportunity to share a meal with another responder as having a powerfully positive impact upon their morale and energy during these difficult times.

Narrative. Many researchers and writers have identified the creation of a chronological verbal and/or graphic narrative as an important ingredient in the healing of traumatic stress, especially intrusive symptoms (Tinnin, 1994; van der Kolk, 1996; Foa et al., 1999). We have found that a creation of a time-line narrative of a caregiving career that identifies the experiences and the clients from which the caregiver developed primary and secondary traumatic stress is invaluable in the resolution of compassion fatigue symptoms, especially those associated with secondary traumatic stress. In the ARP, we instruct the participant/caregiver to "tell your story ... from the beginning—the first experiences in your life that led you toward caregiving—to the present." We use a video camera to record this narrative and ask the caregiver to watch it later that same day, taking care to identify the experiences that have let to any primary and secondary traumatic stress (intrusive symptoms) by constructing a graphic timeline.

In the CCFST, we utilize dyads in which two participants each take a one-hour block of time to verbalize their narrative while the other practices non-anxious "bearing witness" of this narrative.

Desensitization and Reprocessing. With the narrative completed and the identification of historical experiences that are encroaching upon present-day consciousness and functioning in the form of primary and secondary traumatic stress, the caregiver is now ready to resolve these memories. In the ARP, we have utilized Eye Movement Dissociation and Reprocessing (Shapiro, 1989, 1995) as the method-of-choice for this work. In the CCFST, we utilize a hybridized version of a Neuro-Linguistic Programming Anchoring Technique (Baranowsky & Gentry, 1998). Any method that simultaneously employs exposure and relaxation (i.e., reciprocal inhibition) is appropriate for this important cornerstone of treatment. We have had success utilizing Traumatic Incident Reduction (French & Harris, 2000), the anamnesis procedure from the Trauma Recovery Institute (TRI) Method (Tinnin, 1994), or many of the techniques from Cognitive-Behavioral Therapy (Foa & Meadows, 1997; Follette, Ruzek, & Abueg, 1998; Rothbaum, Meadows, Resick, & Foy, 2000). With the successful desensitization and reprocessing of the caregiver's primary and secondary traumatic stress, and the cessation of intrusive symptoms, often comes a concomitant sense of rebirth, joy, and transformation. This important step and ingredient in the treatment of compassion fatigue should not be minimized or overlooked.

In our work with the responders of the Oklahoma City bombing, none reported experiencing intrusive symptoms of secondary and/or primary traumatic stress until several days, weeks, months, and sometimes years after their work at the site. From personal communication with an Incident Commander for a team of mental health responders who worked with over 2,700 victims in New York City the first month after the attacks (Norman, 2002), he indicated that at least one Certified Compassion Fatigue Specialist was available to provide daily debriefing services for every ten (10) responders. He further indicated that if a responder began to report symptoms or show signs of significant traumatic stress they were provided with acute stabilization services by the team and arrangements were made for transportation back home with a referral to a mental health practitioner in the worker's home town. With the intense demands of critical incident work and the paramount importance of worker safety, attempts at desensitization and reprocessing care providers' primary and secondary traumatic stress while on-site seems counterproductive, as they draw from the often already depleted resources of the intervention team.

For this reason, it is recommended that the worker engage in resolving the effects of accumulated traumatic memories only after safely returning to the existing resources and support offered by their family, friends, churches/synagogues, and health care professionals in their hometown.

Self-Supervision. This aspect of treatment is focused upon the correction of distorted and coercive cognitive styles. Distorted thinking may be developmental (i.e., existent prior to a caregiver's career), or may have been developed in response to primary and secondary traumatic stress later in life. Whatever the cause, we have found that once a caregiver contracts the negative symptoms of compassion fatigue, these symptoms will not fully resolve until distorted beliefs about self and the world are in the process of correction. This is especially true for the ways in which we supervise and motivate ourselves. Caregivers recovering from the symptoms of compassion fatigue will need to soften their critical and coercive self talk and shift their motivational styles toward more self-accepting and affirming language and tone if they wish to resolve their compassion fatigue symptoms. For many this is a difficult, tedious, and painstaking breaking-of-bad-habits process than can take years to complete. In the ARP and the CCFST, we have employed an elegant and powerful technique called "video-dialogue" (Holmes & Tinnin, 1996) that accelerates this process significantly. This technique, adapted for use with the ARP, challenges the participant to write a letter to themselves from the perspective of the "Great Supervisor," lavishing upon themselves all the praise, support, and validation that they wish from others. They are then requested to read this letter into the eye of the camera. While watching back the videotape of this letter, the caregiver is asked to "pay attention to any negative or critical thought that thwarts your acceptance of this praise." Then, s/he is instructed to give these critical and negative thoughts a "voice," as these negative thoughts are articulated into the video camera, directed at the caregiver. This back-and-forth argument between the "self" and the "critical voice" of the caregiver continues on videotape until both "sides" begin to see the utility in both perspectives. With this completed, polarities relax, self-criticism softens, and integration is facilitated.

While this technique is powerfully evocative and can rapidly transform self-critical thinking styles, the Cognitive Therapy "triple column technique" (Burns, 1980) that helps identify particular cognitive distortions and challenges a client to rewrite these negative thoughts into ones that are more adaptive and satisfying will also work well for this task. Additionally, as caregivers suffering from compassion fatigue symptoms develop some mastery in resolving these internal polarities with themselves, they are challenged to identify and resolve polarities with significant others.

Individuals traumatized from either primary or secondary sources who are able to "un-freeze" themselves from their polarities, resentments, conflicts, and cut-offs will be rewarded with less anxiety, a heightened sense of comfort inside their own skin, and a greater sense of freedom from the past to pursue their mission of the present and future.

The Crucible of Transformation

Our initial intent in developing the ARP was to simply gather a collection of powerful techniques and experiences that would rapidly ameliorate the suffering from symptoms of compassion fatigue in the lives of caregivers so that they would be able to return to their lives and their work refreshed and renewed. However, as we embarked upon yoking ourselves with the formidable task of sitting across from our peers who were suffering with these symptoms, many of whom were demoralized, hopeless, and desperate, we began to understand that recovery from compassion fatigue required significant changes in the foundational beliefs and lifestyles of the caregiver. As we navigated through the five sessions of the ARP with these suffering professionals we found that most underwent a significant transformation in the way in which they perceived their work and, ultimately, themselves.

Drawing from the work of David Schnarch (1991), who works with enmeshed couples to develop self-validated intimacy and achieve sexual potentials in their marriages, we began to see that many caregivers exhibited a similar form of enmeshment with their *careers*. We found that many of those suffering with compassion fatigue symptoms maintained an other-validated stance in their caregiving work — they were compelled to gain approval and feelings of worth from their clients, supervisors, and peers. In beginning to explore the developmental histories of many of the caregivers with whom we have worked, we found that many carried into their adult lives, and careers, unresolved attachment and developmental issues. For the caregiver who operates from an other-validated stance, clients, supervisors, and peers all represent potential threats when approval is withheld. These perceptions of danger and threat by the caregiver, which are enhanced by secondary traumatic stress contracted in work with trauma survivors, often lead to increased anxiety, feelings of victimization, and a sense of overwhelming powerlessness. As the caregiver is able to evolve toward a more self-validated stance and become more grounded in the non-anxious present, these symptoms begin to permanently dissipate.

Pearlman and Saakvitne (1995) urge therapists to "find self-worth that is not based on their professional achievements. It is essential to develop and nurture spiritual lives outside our work" (p. 396). While we have found no existing empirical data in this ripe area of study, from a treatment perspective we began to see how the symptoms of compassion fatigue make sense in the lives of many professional caregivers, urging them towards maturation.

Instead of viewing the symptoms of compassion fatigue as a pathological condition that requires some external treatment agent or techniques for resolution, we began to see these symptoms as indicators of the need for the professional caregiver to continue his/her development into matured caregiving and self-care styles and practices. From this perspective the symptoms of compassion fatigue can be interpreted as *messages* from what is right, good, and strong within us, rather than indicators of shameful weaknesses, defects, or sickness.

Through our continued working with caregivers suffering the effects of secondary traumatic stress and burnout, we have been able to distill two primary principles of treatment and prevention that lead to a rapid resolution of symptoms and sustained resilience from future symptoms. These two important principles, which have become the underlying goals for our work in the area of compassion fatigue, are: (1) the development and maintenance of intentionality, through a non-anxious presence, in both personal and professional spheres of life, and (2) the development and maintenance of self-validation, especially self-validated caregiving. We have found, in our own practices and with the caregivers that we have treated, that when these principles are followed not only do negative symptoms diminish, but also quality of life is significantly enhanced and refreshed as new perspectives and horizons begin to open.

Suggestions for Compassion Fatigue Prevention and Resiliency

If you or someone you know is experiencing symptoms of compassion fatigue, the following suggestions may be helpful. Please check with your family physician to assure that there are no physical illnesses associated with these symptoms first.

- Become more informed. Read Figley (1995), Stamm (1995), and/or Pearlman and Saakvitne (1995) to learn more about the phenomena of compassion fatigue, vicarious traumatization, and secondary traumatic stress. One book that is especially helpful is *Transforming the Pain: A Workbook on Vicarious Traumatization* by Saakvitne and Perlman (1996).

- Join a Traumatic Stress Study Group. A weekly, biweekly, or monthly meeting of trauma practitioners can become an excellent sanctuary in which caregivers can share (therefore diluting) traumatic stories as well as receive support. Check with the ISTSS (www.istss.org) for a group that may meet in your area or start one of your own. There are several online support resources also. You can find some of these resources through the excellent David Baldwin's Trauma Pages (www.trauma-pages.com) in the "Resources" section.

- Begin an exercise program today (see your physician first). Exercise is one of the most important ingredients to effectively manage stress and anxiety and keeps us buoyant and energized while working with heinous trauma.

- Teach your friends and peers how to support you. Don't rely upon random remarks from friends and colleagues to be helpful. Instead, let them know what is most helpful for you during times of stress and pain. You may choose to offer the same to them in a reciprocally supportive arrangement. Periodic or regular professional supervision may also be helpful, especially during a rough time.

- Develop your spirituality. This is different than going to church, although church may be part of your spirituality. Spirituality is your ability to find comfort, support, and meaning from a power greater than yourself. We have found this quality necessary for the development of self-soothing capacity. Meditation, tai chi, church/synagogue, Native American rituals, journaling, and workshops are all examples of possible ways in which to enhance one's spirituality.

- Bring your life into balance. Remember that your best is ALWAYS good enough. You can only do what you can do, so when you leave the office (after eight hours of work) … leave the office! Perseverating on clients and their situations is not helpful to them, you, or your family. You can most help your clients by refueling and refilling yourself while not at the office. Live your life fully!

- Develop an artistic or sporting discipline. Take lessons and practice as well as play and create. These are integrative and filling experiences. It is paradoxical that when we feel drained that we need to take action instead of sinking into the sedentary "couch potato." Taking action will be rewarded with a greater sense of refreshment and renewal, while activity avoidance will leave us even more vulnerable to the effect of stress the next day.

- Be kind to yourself. If you work with traumatized individuals, families, and/or communities, your life is hard enough already. You do not need to make it more difficult by coercive and critical self-talk. In order to become and remain an effective traumatologist your first responsibility is keeping your instrument in top working condition. Your instrument is YOU, and it needs cared for.

- Seek short-term treatment. A brief treatment with some of the accelerated trauma techniques (i.e., EMDR) can rapidly resolve secondary traumatic stress symptoms. If you would like assistance in finding a Certified Compassion Fatigue Specialist in your area, please contact Compassion Unlimited at (941) 720-0143.

Conclusion

There is little doubt that the extensive efforts being devoted to assisting those affected by the events of September 11, 2001, will have far-reaching influence on the healing of survivors in New York, the people of our nation, and the people of the world. For the first time in the history of our planet, we are beginning to accumulate sufficient knowledge, skills, and resources to facilitate recovery and healing from events such as these. This is not to say that we will not all have painful losses to accommodate or indelible psychological scars—but we will recover. It is a humbling experience to participate, on any level, in this healing.

From our experience with the emergency service workers and professional caregivers who served the survivors of the Murrah building bombing on Oklahoma City since 1995, we also know that there will be casualties in this effort. Many kind and good-hearted emergency service professionals, caregivers, friends, and family members who have witnessed pain, grief, and terror in their service to survivors will themselves end up wrestling with encroaching intrusive images, thoughts, and feelings from these interaction in the weeks, months, and years ahead.

Compassion fatigue is an area of study that is in its infancy. Therefore, very little empirical research has yet been published in this important area. However, the empirical research that does exist and the stories of hundreds of suffering caregivers provides us with evidence that compassion fatigue, and its painful symptoms, are a very real phenomenon (Deutch, 1984; Pearlman & McCann, 1990; Follette et al., 1994; Schauben & Frazier, 1995; Cerney, 1995; Salston, 2000). These symptoms carry with them the potential to disrupt, dissolve, and destroy careers, families, and even lives (many of us grieve the loss of at least one colleague who has committed suicide) and should be treated with great respect. Often, it seems, those who suffer most from compassion fatigue are those individuals who are highly motivated to bring about change and healing in the lives of the suffering. It is especially painful to witness the progressive debilitation of these loving caregivers, who are often our very close friends. Without a doubt, many hundreds, if not thousands, of caregivers and emergency service workers providing hour after hour of intensive and life-altering service to those affected by the events of September Eleventh will experience deleterious effects themselves from this heroic work. Finding the ways and means to both thoroughly study these effects and, maybe more importantly, provide rapidly effective and empirically validated treatment for these suffering heroes, will become a crucial task toward the completion of our nation's healing.

The good news is that the symptoms of compassion fatigue appear to be very responsive to being treated and rapidly ameliorated (Pearlman & Saakvitne, 1995; Gentry & Baranowsky, 1999). While substantially more research in this area will be required before we can offer definitive statements about the nature of treatment, prevention and resiliency with compassion fatigue, some principles and techniques discussed here offer a foundation for helping caregivers resolve their current symptoms and prevent future occurrences. Moreover, we have witnessed that for numerous caregivers the symptoms of compassion fatigue becoming a powerful catalyst for change. With skilled intervention and determination, care providers with compassion fatigue can undergo a profound transformation leaving them more empowered and resilient than they were previously, and therefore better equipped to act as "givers of light."

References

Bercelli, D. (2007). *A bodily approach to trauma recovery.* Retrieved from http://www.traumaprevention. com/index.php?nid=article&article_id=67

Bergin, A. E., & Garfield, S. L. (1994). The effectiveness of psychotherapy. In A. E. Garfield & S. L. Bergin (Eds.), *Handbook of psychotherapy and behavior change* (pp. 143-189). New York: J. Wiley.

Bolman, L., & Deal, T. (2008). *Reframing organizations: Artistry, choice and leadership* (4th ed.). San Francisco, CA: Jossey-Bass.

Bonner, R., & Rich, A. (1988). Negative life stress, social problem-solving self-appraisal, and hopelessness: Implications for suicide research. *Cognitive Therapy and Research, 12*(6), 549-556.

Bloom, S. L. (2000). Our hearts and our hopes are turned to peace: Origins of the International Society for Traumatic Stress Studies. In A. H. Shalev & R. Yehuda (Eds.), *International handbook of human response to trauma* (pp. 27-50). The Plenum series on stress and coping. New York: Kluwer Academic/ Plenum Publishers.

Catherall, D. (1995). Coping with secondary traumatic stress: The importance of the therapist's professional peer group. In B. Stamm (Ed.), *Secondary traumatic stress: Self-care issues for clinicians, researchers, and educators* (pp. 80-92). Lutherville, MD: Sidran Press.

Cerney, M. S. (1995). Treating the "heroic treaters." In C. R. Figley (Ed.), *Compassion fatigue: Coping with secondary traumatic stress disorder in those who treat the traumatized* (pp. 131-148). New York: Brunner/ Mazel.

Cherniss, C. (1980). *Professional burnout in human service organizations.* New York: Praeger.

Danieli, Y. (1982). Psychotherapists' participation in the conspiracy of silence about the Holocaust. *Psychoanalytic Psychology, 1*(1), 23-46.

Deutsch, C. J. (1984). Self-reported sources of stress among psychotherapists. *Professional Psychology: Research & Practice, 15,* 833-845.

Dominguez-Gomez, E., & Rutledge, D. N. (2009). Prevalence of secondary traumatic stress among emergency nurses. *Journal of Emergency Nursing, 35,* 199-204.

Doublet, S. (2000). *The stress myth.* Chesterfield, MO: Science & Humanities Press.

Farber, B. A. (1983). Introduction: A critical perspective on burnout. In B. A. Farber (Ed.) *Stress and burnout in the human service professions* (pp. 1-20). New York: Pergamon Press.

Figley, C. R. (1995a). Beyond the "victim": Secondary traumatic stress. In R. F. Kleber (Ed.), *Beyond trauma: Cultural and societal dynamics* (pp. 75-98). New York: Pelham Press.

Figley, C. R. (1995b). *Compassion fatigue: Coping with secondary traumatic stress disorder in those who treat the traumatized.* New York: Brunner/Mazel.

Figley, C. R. (2002a). Compassion fatigue: Psychotherapists' chronic lack of self-care. *Journal of Clinical Psychology, 58,* 1433-1441.

Figley, C. R. (2002b). *Treating compassion fatigue.* New York: Brunner-Routledge.

Figley, C. R. (2007). *The art and science of caring for others without forgetting self-care.* Retrieved from http://www.giftfromwithin.org/html/artscien.html

Figley, C. R., & Kleber, R. (1995). Beyond the "victim": Secondary traumatic stress. In R. J. Kleber & C. R. Figley (Eds.), *Beyond trauma: Cultural and societal dynamics* (pp. 75–98). Plenum series on stress and coping. New York: Plenum Press.

Figley, C. R., & Stamm, B. H. (1996). Psychometric review of Compassion Fatigue Self Test. In B. H. Stamm (Ed.), *Measurement of stress, trauma and adaptation* (pp. 127-130). Lutherville, MD: Sidran Press.

Flarity, K. (2011). Compassion fatigue. *ENA Connection, 35*(7), 10.

Foa, E. B., Dancu, C. V., Hembree, E. A., Jaycox, L. A., Meadows, E. A., & Street, G. P. (1999). The efficacy of exposure therapy, stress inoculation training and their combination in ameliorating PTSD for female victims of assault. *Journal of Consulting and Clinical Psychology, 67,* 194-200.

Foa, E. B., & Meadows, E. A. (1997). Psychosocial treatments for posttraumatic stress disorder: A critical review. *Annual Review of Psychology, 48,* 449-480.

Folette, V. M., Polusny, M. M., & Milbeck, K. (1994). Mental health and law enforcement professionals: Trauma history, psychological symptoms, and impact of providing services to sexual abuse survivors. *Professional Psychology: Research and Practice, 25*(3), 275-282.

Follette, V. M., Ruzek, J. I., & Abueg, F. R. (1998). *Cognitive behavioral therapies for trauma.* New York: Guilford Press.

Frankl, V. E. (1963). *Man's search for meaning.* New York: Washington Square Press, Simon and Schuster.

French, G. D., & Harris, C. (1998). *Traumatic incident reduction (TIR).* Boca Raton, FL: CRC Press.

Freudenberger, H. (1974). Staff burn-out. *Journal of Social Issues, 30,* 159-165.

Gentry, J. E. (1999). *The trauma recovery scale (TRS): An outcome measure.* Poster presentation at the meeting of the International Society for Traumatic Stress Studies, Miami, FL.

Gentry, J. E. (2000). *Certified compassion fatigue specialist training: Training-as-treatment* (Unpublished dissertation). Florida State University.

Gentry, J. E. (2001). *Traumatology 1002: Brief treatments.* Tampa, FL: International Traumatology Institute.

Gentry, J., & Baranowsky, A. (1998). *Treatment manual for the Accelerated Recovery Program: Set II.* Toronto, Canada: Psych Ink.

Gentry, J. E., & Baranowsky, A. (1999a, November). *Accelerated recovery program for compassion fatigue.* Pre-conference workshop presented at the 15th Annual Meeting of the International Society for Traumatic Stress Studies, Miami, FL.

Gentry, J. E., & Baranowsky, A. B. (1999b). *Compassion satisfaction manual: 1-Day group workshop, Set III-B.* Toronto, Canada: Psych Ink.

Gentry, J. E., & Baranowsky, A. B. (1999c). *Compassion satisfaction manual: 2-Day group retreat, Set III-C.* Toronto, Canada: Psych Ink.

Gentry, J. E., Baranowsky, A., & Dunning, K. (1997, November). *Accelerated recovery program for compassion fatigue.* Paper presented at the meeting of the International Society for Traumatic Stress Studies, Montreal, QB, Canada.

Gentry, J., Baranowsky, A., & Dunning, K. (in press). The accelerated recovery program for compassion fatigue. In C. R. Figley (Ed.), *Compassion fatigue II: Treating compassion fatigue.* New York: Brunner/Mazel.

Gold, S. N., & Faust, J. (2001). The future of trauma practice: visions and aspirations. *Journal of Trauma Practice, 1*(1), 1-15.

Green, R. R., Galambos, C., & Lee, Y. (2004). Resilience theory. *Journal of Human Behavior in the Social Environment, 8*(4), 75-91.

Grosch, W. N., & Olsen, D. C. (1994). Therapist burnout: A self psychology and systems perspective. In W. N. Grosch & D. C. Olsen (Eds.), *When helping starts to hurt: A new look at burnout among psychotherapists* (pp. 439-454). New York: W. W. Norton.

Haley, S. (1974). When the patient reports atrocities. *Archives of General Psychiatry, 39*, 191-196.

Heim, C., Ehlert, U., Hanker, J. P., & Hellhammer, D. H. (1998). Abuse-related posttraumatic stress disorder and alterations of the hypothalamic-pituitary-adrenal axis in women with chronic pelvic pain. *Psychosomatic Medicine, 60*(3), 309-331.

Herman, J. L. (1992). *Trauma and recovery.* New York: Basic Books.

Hooper, C., Craig, J., Janvrin, D. R., Wetsel, M. A., & Reimels, E. (2010). Compassion satisfaction, burnout, and compassion fatigue among emergency nurses compared with nurses in other selected inpatient specialties. *Journal of Emergency Nursing, 36*, 420-427.

Hofman, P. (2009). Addressing compassion fatigue. *Healthcare Executive, 24*, 40-42.

Huggard, P. (2003). Compassion fatigue: how much can I give? *Medical Education, 37*(2), 163-164.
Iacoboni, M. (2009). Imitation, empathy, and mirror neurons. *Annual Review of Psychology, 60*, 653–670.

Joinson, C. R. (1992). Coping with compassion fatigue. *Nursing, 22*(4), 116-122.

Jung, C. G. (1907). The psychology of dementia praecox. In M. Fordham Read, G. Adler, & W. McGuire (Eds.), *The collected works of C. G. Jung,* Vol. 3. Bollingen Series XX. Princeton: Princeton University Press.

Karakashian, M. (1994). Countertransference issues in crisis work with natural disaster victims. *Psychotherapy, 31*(2), 334-341.

Krost, B. (2007). *Understanding and releasing the psoas muscle.* Retrieved from http://www. naturalreflexes.com/pages/Psoas.html

Laposa, J. M., Alden, L. E., & Fullerton, L. M. (2003). Work stress and posttraumatic stress disorder in ED nurses/personnel. *Journal of Emergency Nursing, 29,* 23-28.

Lindy, J. D. (1988). *Vietnam: A casebook.* New York: Brunner/Mazel.

Marmar, C. R., Weiss, D. S., Metzler, T. J., Delucchi, K. L., Best, S. R., & Wentworth, K. A. (1999). Longitudinal course and predictors of continuing distress following critical incident exposure in emergency services personnel. *Journal of Nervous and Mental Disease, 187*(1), 15-22.

Maslach, C. (1976). Burnout. *Human Behavior, 5,* 16-22.

Maslach, C. (1982). Understanding burnout: Definitional issues in analyzing a complex phenomenon. In W. S. Paine (Ed.), *Job stress and burnout: Research, theory and intervention perspectives* (pp. 29-40). Beverly Hills, CA: Sage.

Maslach, C., & Goldberg, J. (1998). Prevention of burnout: New perspectives. *Applied and Preventive Psychology, 7,* 63-74.

Matsakis, A. (1994). *Vietnam wives: Facing the challenges of life with veterans suffering posttraumatic stress.* New York: Basic Books.

McCann, I. L., & Pearlman, L. A. (1990). Vicarious traumatization: A framework for understanding the psychological effects of working with victims. *Journal of Traumatic Stress, 3*(1), 131-149.

McNally, V. (1998, November 7-8). *Training of FBI employee assistance professionals and chaplains.* FBI Headquarters, Washington, DC.

Mitchell, J. (1995). The critical incident stress debriefing (CISD) and the prevention of workrelated traumatic stress among high risk occupational groups. In G. Everly (Ed.), *Psychotraumatology: Key papers and core concepts in post-traumatic stress* (pp. 267-280). New York: Plenum Press.

Norman, J. (2001). The brain, the bucket, and the schwoop. In E. Gentry (Ed.), *Traumatology 1001: Field traumatology training manual* (pp. 34-37). Tampa, FL: International Traumatology Institute.

Pearlman, L. A. (1995). Self-care for trauma therapists: Ameliorating vicarious traumatization. In B. H. Stamm (Ed.), *Secondary traumatic stress: Self-care issues for clinicians, researchers, and educators* (pp. 51-64). Lutherville, MD: Sidran Press.

Pearlman, L. A., & Saakvitne, K. W. (1995). *Trauma and the therapist: Countertransference and vicarious traumatization in psychotherapy with incest survivors.* New York: W.W. Norton.

Perry, B. D. (2007). *Self-regulation: The second core strength.* Retrieved from http://teacher.scholastic. com/professional/bruceperry/self_regulation.htm#bio

Phipps, L. (1998). Stress among doctors and nurses in the emergency department of a general hospital. *Canadian Medical Association Journal, 139,* 375-376.

Pole, N., Best, S. R., Weiss, D. S., Metzler, T. J., Liberman, A. M., Fagan, J., & Marmar, C. R. (2001). Effects of gender and ethnicity on duty-related posttraumatic stress symptoms among urban police officers. *Journal of Nervous and Mental Disease, 189*(7), 442-448.

Porges, S. (1992). Vagal tone: A physiologic marker of stress vulnerability. *Pediatrics, 90*(3), 498-504.

Porges, S. W. (2011). *The polyvagal theory: Neurophysiological foundations of emotions, attachment, communication, and self-regulation.* Norton Series on Interpersonal Neurobiology. New York: W. W. Norton.

Roney, L. (2010). *Compassion satisfaction and compassion fatigue among emergency department registered nurses* (M.S. dissertation). Retrieved October 6, 2011, from Dissertations & Theses: The Sciences and Engineering Collection. (Publication No. AAT 1486171)

Saakvitne, K. W. (1996). *Transforming the pain: A workbook on vicarious traumatization.* New York: Norton.

Salston, M. G. (2000). *Secondary traumatic stress: a study exploring empathy and the exposure to the traumatic material of survivors of community violence* (Doctoral dissertation). Florida State University.

Sabo, B. M. (2006). Compassion fatigue and nursing work: Can we accurately capture the consequences of caring work? *International Journal of Nursing Practice, 12,* 136-142.

Scaer, R. (2001). The neurophysiology of dissociation and chronic disease. *Applied Psychophysiology and Biofeedback, 26*(1), 73-91.

Scaer, R. (2005). *The trauma spectrum: Hidden wounds and human resiliency.* New York: W. W. Norton.

Shapiro, F. (1995). *Eye movement desensitization and reprocessing: Basic principles, protocols and procedures.* New York: Guilford Press.

Stamm, B. H. (1995). *Secondary traumatic stress: Self-care issues for clinicians, researchers, and educators.* Lutherville, MD: Sidran.

Stamm, B. H. (2002). Measuring compassion satisfaction as well as fatigue: Developmental history of compassion satisfaction and fatigue test. In C. R. Figley (Ed.), *Treating compassion fatigue* (pp. 107-119). London, UK: Taylor & Francis.

Stamm, B. H. (2010a). *The ProQOL (Professional Quality of Life Scale: Compassion Satisfaction and Compassion Fatigue)*. Pocatello, ID: ProQOL.org. Retrieved from http://www.proqol.org

Stamm, B. H. (2010b). *The concise ProQOL manual* (2nd ed.). Pocatello, ID: ProQOL.org.

Sussman, M. (1992). *A curious calling: Unconscious motivations for practicing psychotherapy.* New Jersey: Jason Aronson.

Tinnin, L. (1994). *Time-limited trauma therapy: A treatment manual.* Bruceton Mills, WV: Gargoyle Press.

Van der Kolk, B. (1996). The black hole of trauma. In B. A. van der Kolk & A. C. McFarlane (Eds.), *Traumatic stress: The effects of overwhelming experience on mind, body, and society* (pp. 3-23). New York: Guilford Press.

Wilson, J., & Lindy, J. (1994). *Countertransference in the treatment of PTSD.* New York: Guilford Press.

Appendix References

American Psychiatric Association. (1980). *Diagnostic and statistical manual of mental disorders* (3rd ed.). Washington, DC: Author.

Bergin, A. E., & Garfield, S. L. (1994). The effectiveness of psychotherapy. In A. E. Garfield & S. L. Bergin (Eds.), *Handbook of psychotherapy and behavior change* (pp. 143-189). New York: J. Wiley.

Bloom, S. L. (2000). Our hearts and our hopes are turned to peace: Origins of the International Society for Traumatic Stress Studies. In A. H. Shalev & R. Yehuda (Eds.). *International handbook of human response to trauma* (pp. 27-50). The Plenum series on stress and coping. New York: Kluwer Academic/Plenum.

Burns, D. (1980). *Feeling good: The new mood therapy.* New York: Morrow.

Catherall, D. (1995). Coping with secondary traumatic stress: The importance of the therapist's professional peer group. In B. Stamm (Ed.), *Secondary traumatic stress: Self-care issues for clinicians, researchers, and educators* (pp. 80-92). Lutherville, MD: Sidran Press.

Cerney, M. S. (1995). Treating the "heroic treaters." In C. R. Figley (Ed.), *Compassion fatigue: Coping with secondary traumatic stress disorder in those who treat the traumatized* (pp. 131-148). New York: Brunner/ Mazel.

Cherniss, C. (1980). *Professional burnout in human service organizations.* New York: Praeger.

Danieli, Y. (1982). Psychotherapists participation in the conspiracy of silence about the Holocaust. *Psychoanalytic Psychology, 1*(1), 23-46.

Deutsch, C. J. (1984). Self-reported sources of stress among psychotherapists. *Professional Psychology: Research & Practice, 15,* 833-845.

Farber, B. A. (1983). Introduction: A critical perspective on burnout. In B. A. Farber (Ed.) *Stress and burnout in the human service professions* (pp. 1-20). New York: Pergamon Press.

Figley, C. R. (1983). Catastrophe: An overview of family reactions. In C. R. Figley & H. I. McCubbin (Eds.), *Stress and the family, volume II: Coping with catastrophe.*

Figley, C. R. (1988). Toward a field of traumatic stress. *Journal of Traumatic Stress, 1*(1), 3-16.

Figley, C. R. (1995). *Compassion fatigue: Coping with secondary traumatic stress disorder in those who treat the traumatized.* New York: Brunner/Mazel.

Figley, C. R., & Kleber, R. (1995). Beyond the "victim": Secondary traumatic stress. In R. J. Kleber & C. R. Figley (Eds.), *Beyond trauma: Cultural and societal dynamics* (pp. 75-98). Plenum series on stress and coping. New York: Plenum Press.

Figley, C. R., & Stamm, B. H. (1996). Psychometric review of Compassion Fatigue Self Test. In B. H. Stamm (Ed.), *Measurement of stress, trauma and adaptation* (pp. 127-130). Lutherville, MD: Sidran Press.

Foa, E. B., Dancu, C. V., Hembree, E. A., Jaycox, L. A., Meadows, E. A., & Street, G. P. (1999). The efficacy of exposure therapy, stress inoculation training and their combination in ameliorating PTSD for female victims of assault. *Journal of Consulting and Clinical Psychology, 67*, 194-200.

Foa, E. B., & Meadows, E. A. (1997). Psychosocial treatments for posttraumatic stress disorder: A critical review. *Annual Review of Psychology, 48*, 449-480.

Folette, V. M., Polusny, M. M., & Milbeck, K. (1994). Mental health and law enforcement professionals: Trauma history, psychological symptoms, and impact of providing services to sexual abuse survivors. *Professional Psychology: Research and Practice, 25*(3), 275-282.

Follette, V. M., Ruzek, J. I., & Abueg, F. R. (1998). *Cognitive behavioral therapies for trauma.* New York: Guilford Press.

Frankl, V. E. (1963). *Man's search for meaning.* New York: Washington Square Press, Simon and Schuster.

French, G. D., & Harris, C. (1998). *Traumatic incident reduction (TIR).* Boca Raton, FL: CRC Press.

Freudenberger, H. (1974). Staff burn-out. *Journal of Social Issues, 30*, 159-165.

Gentry, J. E. (1999). *The trauma recovery scale (TRS): An outcome measure.* Poster presentation at the meeting of the International Society for Traumatic Stress Studies, Miami, FL.

Gentry, J. E. (2000). *Certified compassion fatigue specialist training: Training-as-treatment* (Unpublished dissertation). Florida State University.

Gentry, J. E. (2001). *Traumatology 1002: Brief treatments.* Tampa, FL: International Traumatology Institute.

Gentry, J., & Baranowsky, A. (1998). *Treatment manual for the Accelerated Recovery Program: Set II.* Toronto, Canada: Psych Ink.

Gentry, J. E., & Baranowsky, A. (1999a, November). *Accelerated recovery program for compassion fatigue.* Pre-conference workshop presented at the 15th Annual Meeting of the International Society for Traumatic Stress Studies, Miami, FL.

Gentry, J. E., & Baranowsky, A. B. (1999b). *Compassion satisfaction manual: 1-Day group workshop, Set III-B.* Toronto, Canada: Psych Ink.

Gentry, J. E., & Baranowsky, A. B. (1999c). *Compassion satisfaction manual: 2-Day group retreat, Set III-C.* Toronto, Canada: Psych Ink.

Gentry, J. E., Baranowsky, A., & Dunning, K. (1997, November). *Accelerated recovery program for compassion fatigue.* Paper presented at the meeting of the International Society for Traumatic Stress Studies, Montreal, QB, Canada.

Gentry, J., Baranowsky, A., & Dunning, K. (in press). The accelerated recovery program for compassion fatigue. In C. R. Figley (Ed.), *Compassion fatigue II: Treating compassion fatigue.* New York: Brunner/Mazel.

Gold, S. N., & Faust, J. (2001). The future of trauma practice: visions and aspirations. *Journal of Trauma Practice, 1*(1), 1-15.

Grosch, W. N., & Olsen, D. C. (1994). Therapist burnout: A self psychology and systems perspective. In W. N. Grosch & D. C. Olsen (Eds.), *When helping starts to hurt: A new look at burnout among psychotherapists* (pp. 439-454). New York: W.W. Norton.

Haley, S. (1974). When the patient reports atrocities. *Archives of General Psychiatry, 39,* 191-196.

Herman, J. L. (1992). *Trauma and recovery.* New York: Basic Books.

Holmes, D., & Tinnin, L. (1995). The problem of auditory hallucinations in combat PTSD. *Traumatology–e: On-line Electronic Journal of Trauma, 1*(2). Retrieved from http://www.fsu.edu/~trauma/art1v1i2.html

Jung, C. G. (1907). The psychology of dementia praecox. In M. Fordham Read, G. Adler, & W. McGuire (Eds.), *The collected works of C.G. Jung,* Vol. 3. Bollingen Series XX. Princeton: Princeton University Press.

Karakashian, M. (1994). Countertransference issues in crisis work with natural disaster victims. *Psychotherapy, 31*(2), 334-341.

Lindy, J. D. (1988). *Vietnam: A casebook.* New York: Brunner/Mazel.

Marmar, C. R., Weiss, D. S., Metzler, T. J., Delucchi, K. L., Best, S. R., & Wentworth, K. A. (1999). Longitudinal course and predictors of continuing distress following critical incident exposure in emergency services personnel. *Journal of Nervous and Mental Disease, 187*(1), 15-22.

Maslach, C. (1976). Burnout. *Human Behavior, 5,* 16-22.

Maslach, C. (1982). Understanding burnout: Definitional issues in analyzing a complex phenomenon. In W. S. Paine (Ed.), *Job stress and burnout: Research, theory and intervention perspectives* (pp. 29-40). Beverly Hills, CA: Sage.

Maslach, C., & Goldberg, J. (1998). Prevention of burnout: New perspectives. *Applied and Preventive Psychology, 7,* 63-74.

Matsakis, A. (1994). *Vietnam wives: Facing the challenges of life with veterans suffering post-traumatic stress.* New York: Basic Books.

McCann, I. L., & Pearlman, L. A. (1990). Vicarious traumatization: A framework for understanding the psychological effects of working with victims. *Journal of Traumatic Stress, 3*(1), 131-149.

McNally, V. (1998, November 7-8). *Training of FBI employee assistance professionals and chaplains.* FBI Headquarters, Washington, DC.

Mitchell, J. (1995). The critical incident stress debriefing (CISD) and the prevention of work-related traumatic stress among high risk occupational groups. In G. Everly (Ed.), *Psychotraumatology: Key papers and core concepts in post-traumatic stress* (pp. 267-280). New York: Plenum Press.

Norman, J. (2001). The brain, the bucket, and the schwoop. In E. Gentry (Ed.), *Traumatology 1001: Field traumatology training manual* (pp. 34-37). Tampa, FL: International Traumatology Institute.

Pearlman, L. A. (1995). Self-care for trauma therapists: Ameliorating vicarious traumatization. In B. H. Stamm (Ed.), *Secondary traumatic stress: Self-care issues for clinicians, researchers, and educators* (pp. 51-64). Lutherville, MD: Sidran Press.

Pearlman, L. A., & Saakvitne, K. W. (1995). *Trauma and the therapist: Countertransference and vicarious traumatization in psychotherapy with incest survivors.* New York: W. W. Norton.

Pole, N., Best, S. R., Weiss, D. S., Metzler, T. J., Liberman, A. M., Fagan, J., & Marmar, C. R. (2001). Effects of gender and ethnicity on duty-related posttraumatic stress symptoms among urban police officers. *Journal of Nervous and Mental Disease, 189*(7), 442-448.

Saakvitne, K. W. (1996). *Transforming the pain: A workbook on vicarious traumatization.* New York: Norton.

Salston, M. D. (1999). *Compassion fatigue: Implications for mental health professionals and trainees* (Defended critical review). Florida State University.

Salston, M. G. (2000). *Secondary traumatic stress: A study exploring empathy and the exposure to the traumatic material of survivors of community violence* (Doctoral dissertation). Florida State University.

Schauben, L. J., & Frazier, P. A. (1995). Vicarious trauma: The effects on female counselors of working with sexual violence survivors. *Psychology of Women Quarterly, 19*, 49-64.

Schnarch, D. M. (1991). *Constructing the sexual crucible: An integration of sexual and marital therapy.* New York: Norton.

Sedgewick, D. (1995). Countertransference from a Jungian perspective (transcript of a lecture given at Grand Rounds to the Department of Psychiatric Medicine, University of Virginia). *The C. G. Jung Page.* Retrieved from http://www.cgjung.com/articles/roundsx.html

Sexton, L. (1999). Vicarious traumatization of counselors and effects on their workplaces. *British Journal of Guidance and Counseling, 27*(3), 393-303.

Shalev, A., Bonne, O., & Eth, S. (1996). Treatment of posttraumatic stress disorder: A review. *Psychosomatic Medicine, 58*(2), 165-182.

Shapiro, F. (1989). Efficacy of the eye movement desensitization procedure: A new treatment for post-traumatic stress disorder. *Journal of Traumatic Stress, 2*(2), 199-223.

Shapiro, F. (1995). *Eye movement desensitization and reprocessing: Basic principles, protocols and procedures.* New York: Guilford Press.

Stamm, B. H. (1995). *Secondary traumatic stress: Self-care issues for clinicians, researchers, and educators.* Lutherville, MD: Sidran.

Sussman, M. (1992). *A curious calling: Unconscious motivations for practicing psychotherapy.* New Jersey: Jason Aronson.

Tinnin, L. (1994). *Time-limited trauma therapy: A treatment manual.* Bruceton Mills, WV: Gargoyle Press.

Van der Kolk, B. (1996). The black hole of trauma. In B. A. van der Kolk & A. C. McFarlane (Eds.), *Traumatic stress: The effects of overwhelming experience on mind, body, and society* (pp. 3-23). New York: Guilford Press.

Wilson, J., & Lindy, J. (1994). *Countertransference in the treatment of PTSD.* New York: Guilford Press.

otes:

Notes:

Notes:

About This Workbook

This workbook is designed for the missions of helping professionals across the world who go to work every day to make the world a better place. They work in high-stress situations at great risk to their personal well-being. This workbook is a guide to preventing and treating compassion fatigue, burnout, and secondary traumatic stress disorder so that they can continue to do their jobs without stress for the rest of their lives!

This workbook is best used with a partner to do the activities with you.